2·88
note
Quality Bks.
n5

This Country Life

This Country Life

Making the most of the simple life
by SAMUEL R. OGDEN

RODALE PRESS, INC.   BOOK DIVISION
Emmaus, Pennsylvania 18049

ISBN 0 - 87857 - 052 - 7

Library of Congress Catalogue Number 72 - 90562

Copyright 1946 by A. S. Barnes & Company

Copyright 1973© by Samuel R. Ogden.

FIRST PRINTING — FEBRUARY 1973

OB-136

PRINTED IN THE U. S. A.

on recycled paper

Portions of this book first appeared in articles in *Vermont Life,*
Organic Gardening and Farming magazine, *The Bennington Banner* and a
previous edition published by A. S. Barnes and Company, New York.

BY THE SAME AUTHOR:

Step-By-Step to Organic Vegetable Growing
How to Grow Food for Your Family
Vermont's Year
America the Vanishing

CONTENTS

FOREWORD

In writing this book I have been motivated by a single purpose, and have hoped to accomplish one thing. During the past forty-two years that we have been living in the country a host of people have passed over our threshold for various reasons and for various lengths of time. Many, in fact most of these people have been from the city, and an astonishing number of them, charmed with the countryside and with our way of life, have bought places nearby for part-time residence. As the years have passed we have heard with increasing frequency the same old question, variously phrased. Generally it runs something like this:

"What do you do to make a living in the country? Of course I know what you do, but you are a special case. What could we do? If only we could be sure of enough to live on, if only our children were educated, if only we could live as you do, we would throw up everything and come to the country to live too. We don't half live in the city. We spend too much and we don't enjoy what we're paying for. Besides that we're always under a strain and a tension. You're the luckiest people in the world if you only knew it. I'd give anything if we could make the break and come to the country to live too."

The purpose of this book is simply to answer that question as best I may. Hearking back to our own situation as we tore out our roots in 1929 and left our established life, and mulling over these questions which have been put to me since living here in Vermont, I have come to the conclusion that the greatest single barrier to the making of the change, is timidity.

Without glossing over difficulties and hazards, I have tried to put into words factual material, experiences and thoughts which would help one to overcome that timidity. I have tried to accomplish this by indicating that there is one principal issue which must be faced, and that issue is the evaluation of what things are most important in life. Like all distressing and difficult decisions the choice is much easier to make if the problem is clearly and simply stated. This I have tried to do.

A lot of people who think that they would like to live in the country are merely enamoured of an idea. They would not actually like what would turn out to be for them grim reality. On the other hand there are many who, if they but had the courage to make the step, would find that life is more satisfying and more fraught with meaning, than they ever imagined that it could be. They would discover with La Rochefoucauld that:

"Happiness lies in our tastes, and not in things themselves; a man is happy in possessing what he likes, not what others like."

While it is true that here he will find no escape from care or grief or even from want, it may be that he will discover that which is infinitely more precious than security of any kind and that is freedom. Not freedom in the realm of things and people, not freedom in the sense of the "Four Freedoms." In fact I suspect that freedom in that particular sense, is but a snare and a delusion, a misleading product of romantic or naturalistic thinking. The freedom which country living promises is freedom of spirit.

> You shall be free indeed not when your days are without care and your nights without a want and a grief, but rather when these things girdle your life, and yet you rise above them naked and unbound.
>
> KAHLIL GIBRAN, *The Prophet*

A great many things have taken place in the quarter of a century since I wrote this book, but with the exception of the need to note new trends in human hopes and aspirations (as well as to add some new cruelties of recent times) this book can stand in all essentials as written. The first chapter stresses some of the new trends, including the new search for Walden which we see among young people today. Part II points out what the changes amount to in a practical sense and asks where we are heading.

SAMUEL R. OGDEN

To Brom and Sully and Hayes and Bill

IN MEMORY OF ARMY DAYS, WHEN WE DISCUSSED SUCH
MATTERS OVER A GLASS OF BEER AT "JOE POLLOCKS"

All that is requisite is that we should pause in living to enjoy life, and should lift up our hearts to things that are pure goods in themselves so that to have found and loved them, whatever else may betide, may remain a happiness that nothing can sully.

GEORGE SANTAYANA

Part One

The most difficult step

THIS BOOK IS ADDRESSED to those who are interested in making a living or a new life in the country. To those who have tried and failed, or those who are making hard weather of it at the moment, or to those who are just beginning, it may offer something of encouragement or assistance. On the other hand, a countryman picking the book up may find that to his knowing eyes, and measured against his lifetime of experience, much that should be included is omitted and much that is included is wrong.

Nevertheless forty-two years of making a living and a new life in the country, after having been born and brought up in the city, have taught me many things, and the conviction that some of the material of my thoughts and experiences may be of value to others has given me the courage to undertake the task.

At first it seemed that the approach to the writing of such a book was one of simple directions, a cataloguing of things to be done, of what to expect, and a statement of experiences—as though one were describing the setting of a muskrat trap, or the making of a set of wrought-iron fire tongs. It soon became apparent that such factual simplicity and directness could not possibly do justice to the subject. When one changes from any other mode of life to country living, profound human values are involved. Such drastic changes can neither be ignored nor treated lightly. In order to be of any value, a study of how to make a living in the country must take into consideration these spiritual and intangible aspects.

What seems to be taking place in our society is a ferment and trek to the country on the part of certain of the young. They do not follow one pattern; but there is one motivation apparently, that governs all the changes. That is escape: An escape is all to the good as long as it is an "escape to" and not merely an "escape from."

It is a search for Walden, so to speak, and it is nothing new. We Ogdens pulled up our city roots (and they were deep ones indeed) as long ago as 1929, and many others—inspired by the writings of Ralph Borsodi —did the same thing. This trend is accelerating now both in Vermont and in other parts of the country, where it has been more extensive and has been going on longer.

In many of the new, so-called "communes" that have been formed it is clear that they are a part of a general pattern of the revolt of youth, of which the more terrifying aspects have been riots and bombings and arson in the cities and disorders and seizures on the campuses and in the classrooms of the colleges.

What seems to be behind the present urge to return to the land is a conviction that our civilization is unendurable, its beliefs false, and its values bankrupt. When we Ogdens came to the country, there were some people who thought of life in an unimproved house back on a dirt road, buffeted by bitter winds and drifted deep with snow in winter, isolated and quiet, as unbearable. There are still some who hope somehow to transplant the cheap distractions of the city to the countryside, and thereby make the country bearable to them. Attitudes and convictions such as these are the outgrowth of a false set of values. If those holding them hope for an adequate reward for their labors, and those hopes are based upon economic and technical conceptions and profit motives, or if their tastes are based on cheap TV and movie excitements, then my sincerest advice is to stay away from the rural life.

Those other people, especially those starting a new life in the communes, know that the ugliness of the cities and suburbia, the mania for speed, the ravishment of the pastoral scene, and above all, the defilement of our environment are what stand behind their revolt. The belief seems to be that if any decency is to return to life, if there is to be any salvation personal or social, materialistic values must be repudiated; greed and envy must be rejected, for from these spring violence, and violence in this cause defeats its own ends.

A recent book, *Famous Long Ago:My Life and Times with the Liberation News Service* by Raymond Mungo of Packer's Corners, Vermont, gives an amusing and well-written account of the transition from violence and dissent in the cities and on the campuses to the bucolic life in a remote corner of Vermont. This again is the search for Walden, and those who seek are in need of help, and are sensibly aware of the fact. There are things these young people will have to know about, simple earthy things, of which as city dwellers they are in complete ignorance.

The earth does not automatically give up her bounty, nor can life be sustained throughout the seasons of the year unless work is sensibly done, and plans are carefully made. In changing over from living at odds with nature in the cities, there is one requirement that seems to be universally accepted, and that is that whatever else happens, the earth and her fruits must be treated organically—that is, within the patterns of nature, without the use of poisons or chemicals.

It has been my good fortune to meet and talk to dozens of kids, all decent, all clean, all serious and all respectfully polite, for my extensive and productive garden is well known locally as an organic garden, and they have sought me out, coming to me for help. It has been a matter of satisfaction to me that they have come, and I am flattered that there is at least one extensive communal garden in this vicinity that is completely the result of information gained from me, even to the varieties planted.

When Helen and Scott Nearing, in 1954, said in their book, *Living the Good Life: How to Live Simply and Sanely in a Troubled World* that they wanted to supply the novice with information that would enable him to "establish and maintain a health-yielding, harmless, and self-contained economy," they stated exactly what the search for Walden is all about. Nevertheless it must be said that the Nearings' definition of the good life is an unusual and extremely austere one, and they have reaped good health and longevity. For one who has the guts to take on the maximum of austerity, there is in this book splendid advice.

No one can really tell anyone else how to make a living at anything. Success in any line of human endeavor certainly depends in the first place upon the conception of success in the mind of the individual. In the second place it depends upon his personal make-up; his health, his helpmeet, his talents, his zeal, his wisdom, and a hundred other attributes too numerous to mention. I choose to add another factor which I am sure cannot be ignored—and that is chance, or fate, or what you will.

Anyone who seriously contemplates living in the country must make his most critical decision at the very outset, and upon this decision rests the fate of his new venture in living. He must decide as to whether or not he is willing to revise drastically his whole scale.of values. This sounds easy, but it is not. It is, in fact, one of the most difficult things that the human spirit can achieve. Involved are habits of behavior and thought, and convictions which are based upon our current philosophies of social science and education.

The ramifications of this accepted standard of values are woven into the very fabric of our national ideology. The recent noticeable flow of population away from farms and from country living has been one result of the acceptance of these values.

The revolt of the young people against these values is more profound and far-reaching than has been recognized. What they demand is a complete rejection of all the old values. Theirs is a revolution of the spirit, having to do with the person, his integrity, his acknowledgment of the presence of evil, his personal resolve to conquer evil within himself, and the acceptance of absolutes, without which such a stand is meaningless.

Our modern emphasis on the importance of material things was evident in the trend of farmers away from the land as early as 1940. In the yearbook of the Department of Agriculture for that year, an explanation was offered:

The farmer today demands a standard of living in keeping with the contribution he makes to the national economy. He sees no reason why he should not enjoy most of those conveniences found in our cities and towns as a matter of course. But to obtain all these things takes money, far more money than farmers forty years ago dreamed of having. Automobiles, tractors, radios, bathtubs, washing machines, refrigerators, etc. must be bought. All of these things are embodied in our national philosophy, a philosophy which might well be termed "Sentimental Materialism." To question this philosophy, to doubt the soundness of these values requires a great deal of courage indeed, yet he who contemplates living in the country must raise these questions and must have this courage.

I saw an example of courage in a group of young people I visited one morning of sun-shot mist after a night of rain in 1970 when my friend Dave Parsons and I spotted the name Mungo on one of a whole cluster of mailboxes at a corner in Guildford, Vt. where four dirt roads come together. We drove in and a tall young man with waving hair and a flowing beard came running down the hill from behind the house. He pleasantly enough wanted to know what we were up to. When Martin, for that was his name, learned who I was and that I wanted to see Raymond Mungo, he was all smiles. I learned later that he ran the communal vegetable garden and that he used my book, *Step by Step to Organic Vegetable Growing* as his guide in the making of it. At this commune the cash to run the establishment comes from literary output rather than from harvests; in fact, they give away all the fruits from their old orchards beyond their own needs, as they do with the vegetables grown in their garden.

People ask whether anyone can make a living on the land, and why it is so many people in recent years have quit trying it.

These questions pierce to the heart of the matter, and my answers can be found in this book.

Two other young people I know are making a try in Oregon. They write:

"Many things have happened since we last saw you. We had no luck finding a farm in Vermont; several things looked good for a while but they always fell through. Then a friend from Oregon contacted us saying he needed a couple to take care of his farm, as he and his wife would be away a lot. In exchange for feeding the animals and general upkeep, we get a house, garden, freezer-use free.

"The place is beautiful, located in the Cascade Mountains. There are 160 acres, maybe 30 acres cleared, house, apple barn, sheds, barn, 5 horses, 13 chickens and a rooster, 4 dogs, 4 cats—whew! We really love it. We planted a 90 by 120 garden and so far everything is doing fine except peppers and melons. I just today started freezing peas. I also plan to can a bunch this year. We have sold organic produce to the local market (lettuce and radishes so far). We should have enough extra to sell all summer, if it works out.

"Later George (not his real name) will work to remodel the apple barn and make it our winter house. It is a lovely rustic building with cedar siding. It will be a cozy house for us. Although we love Vermont and did not want to leave, there came a calling in this direction and it seemed right to make this move west. How long we stay is as yet undetermined, but probably we can stay as long as we like. The area is very beautiful but I miss the hardwood trees.

"Near here is the Hood River valley with its fruit growers association; they spray (with planes) several types of poison, essential in saving their crops (dollars). Meanwhile they pollute the air and all other nearby farms. Fortunately we are far enough away. Then there is the Columbia River, beautiful, but becoming quite lethal to the fish. Also lumber mills line the river."

Though it is possible for young people today to approach the conditions of country living we encountered forty years ago, there are some notable differences. The group where Martin and Ray Mungo live get along, too, without a phone and they hike two miles to get their mail after the deliveries stop with the first snow until mudtime is over in the spring. I sensed that this was a happy and contented place, but Mungo spoke of the fact that their seclusion was being slowly eroded. There are too many jets zooming overhead, and even in summertime, when the leaves are on the trees, at night the garish neons of the nearby town intrude on their solitude.

Our own move to the country stemmed from an event in 1926 when, during a vacation one fall, the idea came to us. My wife and I were snugly ensconced in a luxurious cabin at a club high on the side of Slide Mountain in the Catskills. We were warm and were fed delicious food by a butler who relieved our hosts, as well as the two couples who were their guests, from all aspects of housekeeping. The woods were delightful; there was a tiny brook that discharged its liquid crystal into a pond that lay at our doorstep. None of the other cabins were in view. The season was over, and we were completely alone, isolated from all human contacts, living in the woods beside a pond as Thoreau did, but under circumstances that Henry could not possibly have imagined as he sat in solitude listening to the frogs croak in Walden Pond.

Our time was spent pleasantly enough climbing the mountain and swimming in the icy waters of the pond, and in the evenings there were long discussions before the open fire. One such evening I sounded off, for the difference between this idyllic life in nature's bosom, so to speak, and the stupidities of our suburban living back home really upset me.

I waxed loud and at last one of the girls yelled back at me, "Well, why don't you do something about it besides talk?" "Some day I will," I said, and subsided, but no one believed I would, nor did I myself. But that was the beginning, and in three years from that date my wife and I and our two kids were living in an even more remote wilderness than the one we so enjoyed high up on the side of Slide Mountain.

The move to Vermont in 1929 was the best thing we ever did, and now, looking back over more than forty years marked by their share of tragedy and privations and sorrow, we would not have played it differently for all the tea in China.

With their own hands, at the age of eighty-six, the Nearings are building a stone house in Maine, being nostalgic for the one he left behind when he moved from Vermont. Whether or not the young people returning to the country today will locate Walden, building stone or tar-paper houses for themselves, living lives of serene austerity, no one can predict. Yet if their experiences reveal that what makes life endurable comes from within themselves, not from comforts or possessions, their efforts will not have been in vain, and perhaps the world may be saved by them.

They know that to make a living in the country naturally means to live there, to have a home there. It is the focus of life for each member of the family, a place where all the people and the things dear to a person are assembled. Each has given some of himself to it, both physically and spiritually, and he is part of it. To be warm and dry, to be adequately clothed, to have healthful food, these are necessary; but the goal must be a home and a way of life, not a way to make a living.

The best place to make a living is not in the country, nor has it been since the days of the pioneers. People have been leaving farms for the glamor of the city, its high-speed life and its specialized occupations for over a century. In times of depression, on the other hand, the trend is often in the opposite direction, away from the cities and back to the farms. Let a person figure out why some left the farms, and, further, why some returned; then he can decide as to how badly he wants to try to make a living in the country. If he can agree with Thoreau that modern improvements are improved means to unimproved ends, if he is willing to accept a lower standard of living, if he has the skill and the guts to become a jack-of-all-trades, if he is willing to take on more and harder physical work, and if he is convinced that he can build his own way of life, then he can be sure that he will be immune to those forces that have affected the flow of migration away from the country. And let him study the matter further.

While the material rewards cannot be expected to be great, he who has spirit and vision can build a life more rewarding socially and culturally than he ever dreamed of—a life more full and not possible under city conditions of living, for the fundamental structure of country life must be built by him who lives the life, with almost nothing ready-made for him. The weather and soil are his concern. The processes of nature are his stock in trade. Neither packaged food nor entertainment appeal to him, and neither social intercourse nor culture lie so convenient to his use as they do in the city. The countryman prefers to process his own food, to make his own music, and if he is to have drama, to take part in the theatricals of the community. His recreation tends to be taken simply and directly from the material at hand, from the woods and the waters, the fields and streams. He learns crafts, and what is most important, he must read and think and study if he is to have any ideas.

We are being told all the time that work is a curse, and as he devotes less and less of his time to labor, the happier man's lot will become. We are led to believe the millennium will be at hand when at last man will achieve a life of total leisure, all work being performed by automatic machines. If this seems to be a reasonable and desirable hope, then stay away from the country. The poet Gibran says through the lips of his "Prophet": "And if you work only with distaste, it is better that you should leave your work and sit at the gate of the temple and take alms of those who work with joy." Unless you can agree in essence with the spirit of the above, then it would seem that any hope of building a full and spiritually satisfying life in the country is out of the question. Unless you take up the country life with joy, the move to the country is the most difficult step you could take.

Furthermore, what I have to say is not solely directed to those for whom inflexible rules have left no choice but to seek a different life, but to those as well who want to make a change because of present discontent. Let me make it clear too that the implications of defeat and escape which are sometimes made by the critical arise not from wisdom but from envy. What necessity is there that forces humans to endure a way of life that is unacceptable? To elect to change from unpleasant circumstances to more pleasant ones is to be smart; let no one get away with the implication that in doing this you are a craven who sneaks away from his obligations.

When the time has come to get away from where you are there are lots of possible directions in which to turn; to scenes of childhood, to more pleasant climates, to centers of culture and so on, but which ever way you turn be sure that it is the right way and that you will not regret it later. Once the change has been made it is almost impossible to go back. I have been told that among the saddest people on earth are those who tore out their roots in the east or mid-west only to discover that Southern California is far from being the Paradise they had hoped for, for now they find themselves in an alien land without friends, in a strange setting to which they cannot adjust and with no possibility of return. And this can happen in Vermont just as well as in Los Angeles or St. Petersburg.

Once, a good many years ago, two families of Irish heritage decided to leave the Ozarks where they were established, and move to Vermont. I do not know what glamorous reports they received or how out of all the width and breadth of the United States they landed in this corner of the Green Mountains, but these nice people were here when we arrived back in 1929. In those days there was not much for a farmer to do that would barely keep him alive, and so these people struggled along with their increasing families making increasing demands, but somehow they managed to hang on until after twenty years or so rising real estate values enabled them to sell out and go home. They were fine people, and good neighbors, but they never felt at home here, and now are happy back where they came from.

Farming — a way of life

THOUGH MANY PEOPLE now think of farming as a way of life, not so many years ago there were relatively few who did. When I was called upon to say something on the subject of agriculture during a political campaign several years ago, I referred to farming as a way of life, and contended that many of the current difficulties confronting agriculture were the result of a technique and of procedures which failed to take into account this fact.

The results of this statement were immediate and far-reaching. Farmer acquaintances rose up in their wrath; spokesmen of farm organizations took up the cudgels; and one friend wrote me a long letter undertaking to show me the error of my ways. He said that those who regarded farming as a way of life were not farmers at all. They were people who came to the country to live on their incomes and get away from it all, or to run up losses that could be charged off against their income taxes. All others, like himself, he said, regarded farming as a business proposition, and to hell with farming as a way of life. Some of the publications of the United States Department of Agriculture take the same position.

We met and made friends again, but this incident was the first time that the conflict between the point of view of the commercial farmer and the non-commercial farmer was brought home to me personally. I still maintain that farming can be a way of life, and I mean farming by real farmers with limited capital and no income except what their efforts as farmers bring them.

All of the vacations of my boyhood were spent on the farm of my uncle in northeastern Pennsylvania. Here, from infancy I experienced the ways of country life; I lay under the Snow apple tree in the evening and listened to the mournful cry of the screech owl in the woods across the river and to the comfortable thudding and pawing of the horses in the barn, watching all the while the crazy dance of the lightning bugs up the hill toward the big walnut tree. The labor in the fields was over, the chores were done, a substantial supper of home-cured creamed chipped beef and

13

escalloped potatoes, washed down with copious drafts of cool milk, lay snug in the belly; and all was well with the world.

Uncle Will was a great person, a wise man and a good farmer. He sold maple syrup and honey, potatoes, turnips, apples, eggs, young cattle, and sent milk to the creamery. His small farm included some twenty acres of light bottom land along the small river, another ten acres of stony hillside tillage, and some thirty or forty acres of rocky hilltop pasture land which included a small sugar bush. Some distance away was the "Bear lot" from which he cut his annual supply of fire wood for heating and cooking purposes, and here he pastured his young stock.

The farm—not too good a farm—he had inherited from his father, and he was born in the tiny log cabin which in the early days stood where the chicken house now stands. My grandfather and he, as the oldest boy, built all the buildings now on the place. The buildings are substantial and comprehensive. The house has spring water piped to it from the spring over the hill, and uses its plentiful supply for the first modern bathroom ever to be installed in those parts. The house is snug and warm, centrally heated with a wood burning furnace, its roof always tight, and its exterior always gleaming with a coat of white paint. The spacious front porch runs clear across the front of the house, and shade and privacy are afforded by the Virginia creeper which grows on the columns and trellises.

The front lawn runs down to the dirt road and is ornamented with roses and flower beds which my aunt planted, and is shaded by two magnificent mountain ash trees which my grandfather set out long ago. The road is lined by a double row of enormous and fragrant black locust trees which he also planted. To the left the driveway leads to the house, and then up the hill to the farm buildings. Along this drive as far as the gate, which opens on the paddock enclosure, are apple trees, now old and gnarled, which are also mementoes of my grandfather's wisdom and foresight. Between two of these trees was slung, in the times of my youth, the barrel-slat hammock upon which I used to lie on summer evenings after the day's work was done.

By the paddock gate and not far from the kitchen porch was the stone ice house and milk room, burrowed back into the hill which rises directly behind the house. The front part of this cool and delicious-smelling building was the milk and cool-storage room. Here the cream was separated; here the eggs were washed and stored. Behind a stone partition, and underground, was the ice storage. Here, too, the green of Virginia creeper mottled the gray and white stone walls with shade.

To the left of the ice house and directly behind the house was the kitchen garden, retained at the bottom near the house by a stone wall, wherein the hoptoads lived. A stone walk led up through the garden several hundred feet to the farm buildings, which were grouped around a court, or barnyard. This garden was my aunt's domain, and a goodly portion of its space was devoted to flowers.

Through the paddock gate and to the right, stacked on top of a stone retaining wall under the apple trees, was the wood pile. Beyond this, farther to the right, was the shop building, including the basement, accessible from the front by a flight of stone steps, and open to the air in the rear, the pig pen. Of this delightful place, more later. This building formed the lower right-hand corner of the paddock enclosure.

Next, going up the hill, nestled under a walnut tree was the sugar house, and beyond it the granary. Up the hill, and forming the upper right-hand corner of the enclosure, were the several chicken houses, with the large run which included a small pond, lying to the right. This chicken run, which included several acres, ran up a steep hill that was covered with a grove of black locusts. This grove provided a supply of fence posts, and also shade for the beehives which were scattered up the hillside.

The top of the paddock enclosure was crowned by an enormous flat-topped rock which was completely shaded by a veritable monarch of a sugar maple. It was this tree which gave the place its name of Maple Crest Farm, and it was on this rock that we kids passed many of the happiest moments of our childhood. Here we played house, carved our names, cracked walnuts and butternuts, and from here we surveyed the warm and intimate world of our childhood summers. Down to the gate the close-cropped greensward of the paddock fell away, spotted with white clover, and alive with bees, which I inadvertently stepped on as a barefoot boy. Here the horses grazed after their day's work was done and here I coasted over the close-cropped grass in a wagon in the summer, and on a sled on the occasional visits in the winter.

At the upper left of this enclosure were the barns and the wagon shed. Here were the horse and cow barns with the barn floor and hay mows overhead. Behind the barns was the orchard, with its Pound Sweets, its Sheep Noses, its Baldwins, Russets, Northern Spies, and Greenings. To the right of the orchard the pasture lane led straight to the pasture between stone walls, wherein the chipmunks lived.

After my grandfather's death my uncle never had steady help. He had help by the day as the season required, and he swapped work with his neighbors. My aunt had charge of the chicken department and in later years took over some of the care of the bees. Other than this my uncle did all of the work. Except, of course, that during the summers, from the time I was able to, until the first World War, I helped him. In fact, I left off ploughing for potatoes on the flat to enlist in the army on that memorable day in May, 1917.

My uncle bred and broke his own horses, and he could and did shoe them. He kept his rolling stock and farm machinery in repair himself, and did, besides, all the masonry and carpentry necessary for the upkeep of the place. More than this, he was constantly improving the place, both land and buildings. This in spite of the fact that due to an accident in his youth he had a stiff knee and was partially crippled thereby.

Of all the places on the farm the place I loved best, I think, was the shop. This was a gray boarded structure with lichen-covered shingle roof, a story and a half high, and about 24 by 36 feet in size. As one entered through the double doors, the carpentry department was on the right. A long wooden bench ran along the wall with shelves and tool racks above. At the front end was a tall cupboard with many shelves and drawers.

Herein were nails and screws, bolts and nuts, washers and mowing-machine knives, rivets and fishhooks, lead for sinkers, fishline and bobbers, and ammunition of all kinds—shotgun and rifle shells, powder and primers and loading tools. At the far end of the bench, which included a vise, was my grandfather's big tool chest, with a shelf above it where his molding planes were stacked. This chest contained a complete set of fine carpenter's tools, and in addition such dangerous items as dynamite and fuse, and percussion caps, and his Colt .44 six-shooter.

On the left in front were the stairs which led up above. Beyond that was the metal-working department, the bench along the wall, and the forge and anvil in the far corner.

Overhead were strips between the floor joists, and here were stored an infinite variety of gear. There were bolts of hickory for axe helves, fishing rods, dowel stock, strips of black cherry for furniture repair, fish spears and torches, axe-helve patterns, hoe handles, and, over the forge, various-sized rods and bars and flats of iron and mild steel. In the corner behind the forge was a pile of scrap iron and steel, salvaged from all sorts of places and machines.

Here in this shop I built my first bird house, rigged up my first fishing pole, forged my first turnip-topping knife. Here I learned the use of tools and the care of them, and how to use my hands. Here, too, was the grindstone and emery wheel, and the three-horse-power engine which drove the grinding mill in front of the pig pen downstairs, and also the saw rig which was set up by the wood pile out front. Upstairs were piles of seasoned boards—basswood and curly maple, pine and spruce, ash and oak—along with a miscellaneous assortment of bob sleds, cradles, bee hives, bed steads, hay rakes, and what not.

All the tools and supplies were not there just for fun. They were there for use, and my uncle knew how to use them. There was no farm repair, from mending a broken cutter-bar to making a horse shoe, that he could not do. He could and did build bobs and drays and scoots; and in his spare time, though goodness knows when he found any, he made furniture. One handsome secretary of black cherry and butternut wood I wish I had right now. In addition to all this he was Overseer of the Poor, and Town Trustee. And believe it or not, he took a short nap after dinner each noon.

My uncle, who never had any formal education beyond that afforded by the country school, was always abreast of the latest developments in science, and while I was a student at college he could beat me at knowledge of world affairs. His interests were wide, and his information was amazing, both in scope and degree. He never had the time or the money for travel, which he would have loved. He never owned an automobile. He never spent money for fancy clothes or fine cigars, which he would have enjoyed. There were no vintage wines in his cellar, though there was always a cask of good cider. He was by any material standards a poor man, but he always had room at his table for those who were hungry. He could always contribute to the support of the church, and in a small way to charities. He owned his farm; and he had a small savings account in the bank, against a rainy day. He lived a full, rich, and useful life. He brought comfort and help to many. He was a wise and dignified man, one to be recognized as such in any set of circumstances, amongst any gathering in the world. He was a farmer, and I submit that his farming constituted a way of life—not a way to make a living.

It can be said, I suppose, tnat all I have said on the subject of my uncle's farming represents an era that is gone and that such a way of life is no longer possible. Perhaps; but if the ideal life is thought of as including the minimum of labor, if success is measured in terms of material possessions, if human satisfactions are dependent solely upon material comforts and mechanical devices, then I am wrong and farming or living in the country is not a way of life. When it becomes merely a way of making a living—and a poor way at that—those who do choose to live on a farm are placing their hopes for success upon governmental subsidies and legislative action. Their profits will be forced at the expense of the more affluent dwellers in congested cities.

There are many dangers inherent in the commercial point of view. I have no faith that country life can be based upon city standards, and there is plenty of historical evidence to indicate that the commercial farmer is ever at the mercy of factors beyond his control. Agricultural activities which are based solely upon profit motives inevitably end up with glutted markets and impoverished and poisoned soil. The glut is obvious in the need for the subsidy program. The impoverished soil is evident wherever dust bowls and erosion have laid waste the land. The poisoning of the land with hard pesticide sprays has become evident in contaminations of food chains and depletion of birds and other organisms high on the food chain.

For the past forty years I have lived in the country, and I have made a living here—though not by farming. In fact, where I live, in a mountainous high-altitude region, the land is not ideally adapted to farming. Some of my neighbors do farm; I have a garden, sell produce, and have additional occupations.

Every April, though there is still snow, I begin my gardening by opening the coldframes to let in some sun. One year, in spite of only scant snowfall I still was forced to travel out back to take care of them on snowshoes. By the end of the month the snow disappears and I plant sweet peas and set out the onion plants which I order by mail from Texas. By early May if we have a warm day, some of the seeds poke up, and since these early plants are hardy, the May frosts do not harm them.

After that I keep on planting like mad, for there is a lot to be done in our large and productive garden. And the process continues into July, so to get the seeds of the frost-resistant vegetables in early is a must.

We begin to eat scallions from our top-multiplying onions by May 8th, and on the 13th, in an average year, we have our first taste of asparagus. If I am encouraged then by a succession of fine days, I plant beans (under caps) and as an experiment put in two rows of corn, being prepared to sacrifice this much on the altar of an early crop, if necessary.

Then hundreds of plants are moved from the coldframe out into the garden to stand in lovely rows of green. If there is a rainy spell in the meantime, things will explode, and the first plantings of peas grow up three inches above ground. By about the 20th of May we have tiny lettuce thinnings to eat roots and all, perfectly delicious in their bath of olive oil with a touch of salt, pepper and vinegar. In a few days we have a second batch mixed with spinach thinnings and a few tiny radishes.

When these plantings come up, they look mighty fine and brave, green against the rich chocolate-colored earth. At this time of year, one real hard freeze would ruin us, but I hope for the best (laugh if you choose) because of the phases of the moon. I have a theory which I suppose will be classified by some as rather a superstition, and that is that the cold frosty nights are more likely to occur at the time of the full moon. In late May, therefore, I plant corn at the time of the last quarter and look forward to their escaping unharmed when the temperature falls into the low 30s.

My garden has become an attraction to a growing number of young people who are turning to the soil in their effort to gain realistic relationship with life. They have been here, many of them, to talk with me, and from them I have received a renewal of hope. In their search they will find beauty and health, and any help I give would seem to me to be about the most rewarding thing I could possibly do.

These new farmers and my neighbors who made a living by farming thirty years ago bear out my conclusions about commercial farming versus farming as a way of life.

Farming can be either an industry or a way of life. If it is an industry it needs to be run like an industry, with capital, with cost accounting, with science, with organized attempts to constantly broaden the market, and so to profitably cheapen the product by rationalization. But the farmer when he has a soil factory and not a farm, want to be treated as an agrarian. He asks to be considered as the backbone of the nation. He holds himself out to be the figment of Jefferson's dream, when as a matter of fact he is a speculative business man.

After all, who can say that it may not be wise to look back upon the olden times, even though the days to which I refer on my uncle's farm are not so olden. Modern science has substituted exact rules for this and that, for feeding and fertilizing, but I wonder if it can substitute exact rules for old-time wisdom and ways of life. In any event, while farming can surely be regarded as an industry and practiced as such, the one who does this will find much more exacting regulations imposed on him, and his competitive position made much more hazardous by the intervention of nature. These are reasons that farming as commercial enterprise is always precarious, and often seeking for subsidy.

The Year Books of the United States Department of Agriculture are ponderous tomes of some twelve hundred pages or more. They are the official expression of the Department of Agriculture and epitomize the point of view of farming as an industry. Justifications, theories and expediencies can be found in them—theories that are based exclusively upon the profit motive in farming, and upon the assumption that farming is exclusively an industry and nothing else. This is, I believe, the high spot in our wrong thinking about agricultural matters, and a most obvious example of how far afield adherence to false values can lead us in both thinking and living. Specifically, if farming is exclusively a commercial venture, an industry and nothing else, how then can governmental subsidies in cash and kind be justified unless all other types of commercial enterprises from abattoirs to xylophone manufacturers be treated with this same paternal care and be offered these same benefits?

Experts writing for the USDA year books make such statements as:

"However it cannot be over-emphasized that hand labor competing with more efficient machine methods on other farms and in other areas will bring very low returns for the effort expended, and both the individuals concerned and society as a whole would benefit if more productive employment could be found."

In this statement you will note three things: first, that there is an assumption that labor as such is a curse; second, that material profit is a necessary concomitant of labor; and third, that one who labors without material profit is an object of concern for society. These conceptions, if carried through to their logical conclusion, will give every one of us cause to think.

Another agricultural economist, making a study of "Land Utilization as a Basis for Economic Organization," speaking of the financial balance sheets of 128 farm operators, studied in Vermont in 1929 says, "These figures present no record of affluence achieved. Affluence, however, is relative to needs and desires, and those who gain little may enjoy much."

These two statements, it seems to me, sum up the differing points of view, as well as can be done in few words. If you agree with the first, my advice to you is to stay away from farming and from country living; if you agree with the second, and are willing to take a chance, you are ready for country life, for the first steps to attain it, and the first difficulties you will meet.

The family in the country

IN SPITE OF REPEATED STEPS taken to break it down, the family is still the basic unit of our civilization—whether it be a group of people related by blood, or by choice, living as a unit. Some of the tendencies towards breaking down family life are the inclination of parents to shift their proper responsibilities toward their children to others—to schools, to groups, and even to social and law-enforcement agencies. This is accentuated by the way we live in cities, in congested, spaceless living conditions. One writer on the subject of country living attributes his change of residence from the city to the country to the fact that if a city apartment was no place to keep a dog, it was certainly no place to raise children.

If you live in the country, you can make up your mind that the home is the most important thing in the whole scheme of things. It is more important than anything, mortgage interest or mastitis, drought or tornado, more important even than any individual in the family or out. If you are willing to accept this as the truth, and if you think you have the patience and the understanding required to build a happy and self-sufficient home, then you are ready to try living in the country.

Almost everyone who spent his childhood on a farm cherishes the dream that when he has made his pile he will return. He is willing to deprive his own children of that heritage which he himself treasures so highly, because of the exigencies of the moment, because of the necessity of making money. He rationalizes his position to himself by thinking of the educational and cultural advantages which city life offers his children. Of which more later. In any event, whatever the actual reasons may be, he cherishes, through a romantic golden mist, memories of barefoot childhood days down on the farm; memories of juicy apples on a frosty October morning; memories of the track of a rabbit in the new-fallen snow down by the brook, memories of box traps, and sling shots, and the swimming hole under the willow tree. He remembers his boyhood and family life on the farm with pleasure, and he looks forward to the day when he can return. But somehow or somewhere there is a break with reality; the ideal cannot be achieved.

This divergence between the ideal and the actual is common enough, but the fact remains that there is a good deal to be said in favor of bringing up children in the country. For here, the home itself is the main thing. It is a composite of many spiritual and material things, and its importance rests on the basic conditions of country living. By the very nature of this life the home occupies a large place in the daily existence of the members of the family; and by the same token it can be a very wonderful place indeed, or a place to get out of as soon as possible.

In the city a family can, and often does, get along without a home at all. The place where the family lives is no more than a place to hang one's hat, a place to sleep, an address for mail and telephone service. The more the small tasks of daily living like those providing food and warmth are performed mechanically, or by outsiders for hire, the less is there any home life. And what is worse, if there is no real homelife, the smaller and smaller tasks of daily living become more and more burdensome to those who perform them. Then a vicious circle is set up and outside distractions and cheap excitements and amusements mean that even less time is devoted to the making of a home; and the less homelike the house becomes, the less interest any member of the family has in being there. Apparently satisfactory substitutes arise: eating in restaurants, or TV dinners; social activities at the corner store, in a parked car, or in the movies; and reading is taken care of by tabloids, picture magazines, comics, TV and the movies.

In the country this is not so. If the necessary shift in fundamental values has been made, the most satisfying and happiest family life can be had in the country. This for several reasons. In the country there is more living room. The story-and-a-half cottage in which we live, and which was built over a hundred years ago by a farmer of very modest means can sleep fourteen people. There are two living rooms, one of which in former days was the parlor, so that while the old folks read or chat in their end of the house the young ones can have their games and music and gaiety in the other end of the house. Each can have his own quarters, and room to store his gear. More than in the city there is room in which to move around, there is space where personalities can expand. We all need room if we are to be happy, and in this era of faster and faster population growth, the craving for room is becoming intense. In the country the poorest can have it, and usually the house is larger and more spacious. The domain of no member of the family, moreover, is limited to the house. Everyone's activities overflow the house and spill into the outbuildings and outdoors.

To own the land is something of a satisfaction, but more than this, one's occupations and interests are spread out onto the land, in gardens and orchards and fields. The housewife has her gardens, the old man has his shop and his barns, the children have their outside activities which are private projects of their own. Their living space is large, and because of this largeness, egos seem to diminish, all of which seems to make for happy and smooth-running family life.

Having enough room so that each can get out of the other's way works well for family harmony; and yet in the country the members of the family are together more than they are in the city. And this, paradoxical as it may seem, also works for family unity.

Then too, the necessity of each member of the family sharing in some part of the chores of daily living gives each an understanding of team work, and of the interdependence of each upon the other. The house has to be kept tight and dry, the wood must be cut if there are wood stoves for cooking and heating, then it must be sawed and split, and the wood box kept filled. The food has to be grown, and the garden tended. The produce of the garden must be gathered, and preserved or stored for family use. There is canning and preserving to be done. All this in addition to the regular household duties of cooking and cleaning and washing. Each member of the family has the responsibility of performing one or several of these tasks, almost from infancy, and the result is the feeling of being a useful part of the family machine.

Those who fail in country living fail because they have been unwilling or unable to change their point of view or reevaluate their sense of what is important. Questions of making a living, of education for the children, of self-sufficiency and of comfort and culture all enter the picture, but there are also practical problems, too. Rotted timbers, smoking stove pipes, frozen water pipes, leaky roofs, hazardous winter travel, garbage disposal, and a hundred other problems can affect the atmosphere of family life.

Let there be no misunderstanding—just to live in the country will produce no utopia of family life. Dyspeptic grouches and temperamental tizzies are to be found wherever humans gather, whether in families or board meetings, from the North Pole to the South Seas. I know of one farm family composed mostly of boys, and a goodly number of them too, whose affairs never seemed to move ahead the way they should—with all the manpower that was available. The boys would stand outside the barn and argue as to whose turn it was to milk, until the cows could have been milked twice over. In fact the affairs of this particular family seemed to go from bad to worse until the war came along, leaving the oldest boy home alone with his father. From this moment things changed. The herd has been increased and improved, the farm work is done on schedule, and all of this with fewer hands. No, there is no guarantee of peace and harmony, but the chances for a well-rounded, integrated family life are greater in the country than in the city, for the reasons that I have mentioned.

The effect of family living has been apparent in the changes we have seen in several city children who have been sent to stay with us for protracted visits. I use these children as examples, rather than our own, because the change in their behavior could be watched. Our children have scarcely ever used the radio, never used television, and seldom went to the movies; they have taken hunting and fishing, snowshoeing and skiing very much for granted.

These other children, though, when they first come, all have *their* radio or TV programs to which they *must* listen. The very heavens would fall if they missed one episode of "Superman" or "Man from U.N.C.L.E."

It is as though their lives were oriented to these programs, as if by instinct they knew the exact moments when these programs are on. There you will find them, glued to the speaker or the screen. (This *may* be fine; the advantages or dangers of this type of occupation for children have no place for discussion here.) After one week of country life, however, the child loses absolutely all his interest in such programs, and the radio or TV passes out of his life as though it never had existed.

As far as family life is concerned this is to the good. The occupations which the child has substituted for the radio and television are just as enthralling, if not more so, than the old, and just as hard to distract him from. But there is this difference: instead of being taken up by an unreal, imaginary excitement, the child is now occupied with realities. And for this reason he is a better person to live with.

If the child has been accustomed to going to the movies, he soon gets over the preoccupation with movies as a basic item in his activities. Swimming and fishing and all the animal life of the country, along with all the winter activities of sledding and skating and skiing as well as making tunnels in the snow and snow houses make exciting forms of occupation that keep the days full and happy without need for other excitements. As before, this makes for better home conditions and for happier family life.

Happy family life is based upon mutual understanding and affection, and requires leadership and forbearance. Except in rare instances the original affection of each member of the family for the other can be taken for granted. Understanding, however, is another matter. Love and affection can carry the family ship through many a storm, which, had there been understanding, never would have occurred. Storms there inevitably will be, but though it is a truism to state it, the fewer storms the better. And so the need for understanding is great. Love and affection are not enough, nor is it enough that understanding be added, for along with understanding must go forbearance. To understand another's perplexities is all right as long as one is not personally affected by the situation; but when we ourselves are affected by another's perplexities, it is quite apt to be to our annoyance. And so the need for forbearance.

Furthermore, the family is a group, but at the same time it is an entity. As such it must have a direction, a reason for being, a common belief and a common goal toward which each one and all together strive. Without this unity and common ideal there can be no such thing as real family life. And no group, however small, be they ever so well-intentioned, can ever move together toward a common goal without a leader. Though the romantic individualism which is the basis of our national philosophy, our sentimental materialism, insists that each one of us is an individual with a will just as important as the will of any other, old, wise, young or stupid, there is plenty of historical evidence to show that any group, however unifying their ideals, must fail of their objective unless some individuality is surrendered and leadership accepted. How this leadership is assumed in a family does not particularly matter. Wisdom and character and experience should form a background for leadership, and I may point out that these attributes are seldom possessed in any great degree by a child.

My belief is that the conditions of country living do, for the most part, promote understanding and affection, and forbearance and leadership as well. To be away from the artificial stimulations and excitements of city life, to be close to the majestic and inexorable operations of nature, tends to develop patience and forbearance and understanding. Farming and craft occupations mean that the parents spend more time with the children, and that they spend more time with each other than in the city. This promotes family solidarity and loyalty. Moreover, the necessity of struggling with nature promotes self-sufficiency and serenity in ways no other occupation can do. It also promotes a willingness both to assume and to accept leadership.

It is for all these reasons that family life takes on an importance in the country that it may not have in the city. A feeling for the importance of family life and an understanding of its importance are necessities if you are going to live in the country. When you are willing to accept these necessities, you will find that the best place in all the world to bring up a family is in the country.

The conviction that such an attempt to return to the land constitutes an "age-old American myth"—as claimed by Richard Sennett in his New York Times review of Raymond Mungo's *Total Loss Farm* has been proven false times enough. In fact, I would now say that unless the return becomes universally adopted, the culture of our society will crash to a grinding halt. Joseph Wood Krutch, speaking of Thoreau's Walden venture, said: "But for Thoreau himself this was not an escape from, but an escape into reality." A distinction must be made between those who escape "from" and those who escape "to," and the escape "into reality" describes well enough the situation of many who are moving to the country in this century as well as those who moved in the last.

If the habitation you make in the country is not a home, it is a hell, and the only way to avoid stark tragedy is to go away. So if you are to live in the country, you can make up your mind that the home is the most important thing in the whole scheme of things. It is more important than anything, more important even than any individual in the family or out. If you are willing to accept this as the truth, and if you think you have the patience and understanding required to build a happy and self-sufficient home, then you are ready to try living in the country.

Country community life

IN THE CITIES, along with the diminishing of the importance of family life, there has come about an attendant lack of interest in community affairs. The reasons for this are several. During the past hundred years in this country there has been a definite population trend away from rural districts, from the small towns and villages, toward the big cities. As a consequence the larger cities have grown tremendously, and their populations have become composed of people without roots. Their physical growth has outstripped their spiritual growth; and what is more, in their spread they have engulfed smaller, surrounding communities, more or less wiping out the community aspects of each in the process.

Shopping habits and the greatly increased tempo of travel, both by land and air, have meant that many citizens of smaller communities tend to travel to the large cities for their shopping and also for their recreation. The discount houses that ring both large and small cities draw bargain-hunters from villages. The village store is no longer the center of activity it used to be.

Mere size in itself is another factor. Plato has said that the ideal limit in size for a governing unit is ten thousand citizens; and surely the same figure applies to communities as such. The way people live in apartment houses and multiple-unit housing tends to destroy all feeling of neighborliness, or even a knowledge of who one's neighbors are unless one belongs to a block association.

With the disappearance of the community spirit, something very worthwhile has disappeared from our national life. For the most part such vestiges of community life and spirit as remain will be found in the rural districts, and in the main all hope for its rebirth lies here. Community living requires active participation on the part of the individual, but the returns to the individual are out of all proportion to the effort expended. High morale is a condition greatly to be desired and concerted community effort is an indication of high morale. Spruce appearance is a sign of it, and neat grounds, well-painted houses, cared-for road-sides; and evidences of time and thought spent on the schools and churches are all signs of high community spirit and morale.

To the city dweller who is thinking of changing to country ways of living, these are the things to be on the watch for and should be important factors in making his decision as to where to live. Are the villages surrounded by gas stations and shopping centers, with hamburger stands on every other corner, or are there signs that the villagers here did not succumb to such commercialism?

Nevertheless the lack of evidences of community spirit should not deter one unduly. After all, the conditions for the development of community action can turn out to be ideal in the country when people there live with nature and live from the land. Good will and a fresh point of view from a newcomer can sometimes accomplish wonders, after the people get to know who you are.

When we landed in the little mountain community which was to be our home for the next forty years the first gathering of the townspeople to which we were introduced was Town Meeting, held in March shortly after we appeared on the scene. It was a bright sunny day, overhead a sky of deepest azure blue, and all around the ground was covered with snow; the bare road was shining with puddles and deep with mud, and here and there in the fields the good old earth was beginning to show through the blanket of snow. Outside all was vibrant with light and with the promise of life about to burst forth. There was a happy hint of spring in the mild air and in the blue of the sky. Inside it was a different story indeed. Sour faces regarded one another across the gloomy hall. Personal feuds which had been fermenting during the short shut-in days and the long lonesome nights of the winter were boiling over in the discussions. Bitter words were spoken and personal animosities were aired with great gusto. The business of the town was accomplished, but in the doing barriers against community action were set up, and as a result of personal grievances, those who were most qualified to act as town fathers refused to accept any responsibility or town office. There were not many people there, and there were not many offices to fill, but the barriers were up and they refused to budge.

While this meeting was evidently in the tradition of meetings in the past, it was a great shock to my wife and me. When we talked it over, we came to the conclusion that the lack of cooperation and bitterness was not a result of the clash of irreconcilable personalities, but rather the result of a disagreeable mood, and that this mood was induced by the shut-in life of the winter past and was fostered by peeves and grudges which had carried over from other disagreeable Town Meetings. During the course of deliberations time for lunch approached, and when the hour struck each one hied himself off to his corner, or off home, to eat his own lunch silently by himself. Having noticed this, and further that some of the lunches were pretty drab and tasteless affairs, my wife decided that it would be a good thing if she got busy before next Town Meeting and organized a community social lunch for the occasion. When the time came and she proposed the idea, to her great surprise it was welcomed with enthusiasm on all sides, and preparations went forward with great good will.

Committees were formed, the women baked together, the men took more interest in what was happening than they intended to, and the Town Meeting of the next year made a complete and thorough break with the past. It set an example, moreover, that has been followed in this village many times ever since.

In other communities across the country the volunteer participation of newcomers has had a leavening effect. Though the newcomer is likely to find himself regarded as an outsider at first, and looked on with suspicion, if he is accepted or if his ideas are found helpful, he may move beyond the special set of conditions reserved for "city folks." He may even be asked to perform certain roles in town affairs or he may even be elected to office.

In our village, as a result of the new temper, there has arisen a pride in local town affairs, a new willingness to share in the responsibilities of government of the town—not for what can be got out of it, but for the good of the people.

The concrete results of this new attitude were as incredible as the change in temper itself. A few of them that arose during the early years were: a new school and playground; church repainted; cemetery fenced; snow removal equipment purchased; improved condition of roads both winter and summer; complete disappearance of the town debt; a lowering of the poor costs, in fact of all the costs of local government except schools; and most noticeable of all, a decided change for the better in the appearance of the town itself.

The opportunity to participate in community affairs exists no doubt wherever humans foregather, but certainly the ideal field for such activity is in the country, and to be a part of it, even a tiny part, makes life a better thing. For fear of being misunderstood I want to make it clear that the above is not to be construed as a brief for "good works." Community solidarity cannot be imposed from the outside. No "foreigner" or stranger, no youth worker or social agency worker can effect any worthwhile accomplishment as long as the people think of him as being on the outside. It is strictly an inside job, and each newcomer must first become a member of the community—no matter how long it takes—before he qualifies for any of the benefits of belonging. In some areas it takes longer than in others and it sometimes depends on such minor details as the accent you speak in or the way you wear your hair. It can never be achieved by a feeling of superiority or condescension nor by "good works."

In several parts of the country any newcomer to a rural community is going to be regarded as an outsider, especially if he comes from the city. In parts of New England this at first can seem like an insurmountable barrier; in other areas, however, there is often a warmth of greeting which is surprising, especially if the newcomer is young and obviously in need of assistance.

When a newcomer arrives in our town, he is definitely on probation, and he remains so, unaccepted or merely tolerated, until some subtle change occurs. Maybe they have seen him chopping wood, or digging in the dirt, or helping someone get his car out of a snowbank. But in any case, it seems safe to say that kindliness, patience and understanding along with tolerance and modesty will break down the barriers more easily than will superiority and arrogance. However self-sufficient one may be, however sure he is that he is not dependent on others, he will fail to receive the greatest benefits of country living if he fails to pass the test and remains an outsider.

Once accepted, however, the very fact that he comes from the outside, and brings with him a fresh point of view, gives him greater opportunities; and from personal experience I can state that the greatest rewards that living in the country has to offer come from the exercising of these opportunities.

One writer on country living recognizes this hostility on the part of the native to the outsider and accepts it as a challenge. After a year of living in the country he refers to his neighbors as "natives," and the context is such that the reader can catch the inflection of a sneer in the word. His reaction to the challenge is to organize an invasion to the end that some day he and the other newcomers will outnumber the "natives." This invasion worries the "natives" of course, much to the author's satisfaction. The successful end of his campaign arrives when by virtue of the numbers of his kind he can say, "This part of the United States is as much ours as it is yours."

This represents a point of view which I am afraid is fairly widespread. It is a point of view which places class distinctions above human ones, and if it is held by a prospective country dweller my advice to him is to give up ideas of living in the country, at least until such time as he can organize a mass invasion. Should that happy day arrive, and should he and his cohorts be able to take over a section of the countryside en masse, he still will have missed the best part of country living.

The opportunities for participation in community affairs are as numerous as the kinds of community activities there are and the kinds of neighborly activities. Besides school and church activities, and participation in town planning or town governmental affairs, we have dug potatoes for a sick neighbor, we have built a house for an impoverished family whose house was destroyed by fire, and many a time we have all pitched in to help when a neighbor's crop has been threatened with destruction. In the old days we also brought in wood for the aged.

In our town of Landgrove the population has fluctuated considerably since 1929 when we came here. According to the 1930 census, there were 104 people here, but that dropped to 64 in 1940 before it rose again to 80 in 1950. By 1960 it was down to 49, and then rose right back up to the 1930 figure of 104 in 1970. In the previous century, however, Landgrove was larger; in 1900 there were 225 people, and in 1880 there were 246. Ups and downs like these have been characteristic of many small places throughout the the nation.

In such a sparsely settled place, the church has slender support from a very small congregation, and it is usually so small that it is only possible to hold services in the summer time. In spite of this, however, at one time in the 'thirties, the community fund started to procure a new school-house for Landgrove grew large enough to provide funds for giving the church a new coat of paint when needed, and even encouraged plans for the landscaping of the churchyard.

In New England towns where almost all the inhabitants belong to the same church and send their children to the same school, there is the added community force in the Town Meeting government. In other areas where the County form of government is the norm, there is nothing like this New England community force. Voluntary associations for recreation, community betterment or youth programs sometimes take its place or the PTA where school matters are a prime concern.

The town, here, is the basic unity of government in the state. And each town, as both a geographic and governmental subdivision of the state, is responsible for making its own tax rate, its own "grand list" for tax purposes, and for the maintenance of its town roads and, until recently, its poor. The schools are run by a school board, and taxes for the maintenance of the schools are levied by the school district, which in the case of sparsely-populated towns coincides with the town area itself. In recent years, there has also been state aid for schools, but local school taxes are still based here on property valuations. These valuations are made by local town listers who make the appraisals which are entered in the grand list. Following a basic formula the town itself at its Town Meeting sets the tax rate at a figure sufficient to cover the costs of town operation. The selectmen, usually three but in some towns five, are the governing board of the town. The road commissioner in towns where there is no town manager has charge of the roads, and until recently the overseer of the poor had the care of the town poor assigned to him.

Gradually the newcomer finds himself accepted by his townspeople. After he has helped mend a neighbor's tractor, and his wife has helped in a nursery school, after they have given people rides to other towns or taken children in a car pool, and have shown the townspeople they are willing to work in the soil like everyone else, they begin to be accepted. Later, when the newcomer has proven himself by his participation in community affairs, and by the wise management of his own business that he is a sound person, the call to act in some official capacity may come to him. He might become moderator of the Town Meeting, or act as one of the listers, or a call might come to him from one of the caucuses to run for selectman or town or district representative. In recent years newcomers have often been asked in various towns to join either the local or regional planning commission and contribute from their experience in other places.

Now as a member of a small rural community he has an opportunity to bear a small part of the load of government, which as a city dweller he would probably never have. And this without participating in politics or being a politician in the current meaning of the word.

The closer the machinery of government is to the people, the more meaning it has; and the more active the participation in the responsibilities of government, the better the citizen. For these reasons, living in the country, or in a small rural community, brings one to better citizenship.

This opportunity to become a member of a community and to get close to or even into the workings of the governing of the community is one of the strongest reasons for a return to the country. Living in the country does not necessarily lead to elective office or community leadership, but the opportunities are there to a degree not found in the city. Anyone who cares to look at the record can see that in 1945-6 roughly 10 per cent of the members of the House of Representatives in the Vermont Assembly were city born and bred—persons from the big cities outside the boundaries of the state, who have come to the country to live and who have accepted their responsibilities as leaders in their communities.

Another matter of concern to those who contemplate living in the country is the matter of health and of medical facilities. Though many families have little traffic with the medics, and have good healthy children, available health care is something a newcomer likes to know about. In the past there have been indications that care of eyes and teeth has not been up to par; modern facilities and school inspections have been greatly improved in many parts of the country. There are good modern hospitals in the medium-sized cities all across the continent, and excellent rescue squads made up of volunteers who will take sick people to the hospital. There are specialists in many places, among them doctors who themselves have given up city life to move to more rural areas to bring up their children. There used to be widespread shortages of general practitioners in rural areas, but one has begun to hear that in a town here or in a town there the general family doctor is coming back. In Vermont we have good men now all across the state, and there is no spot in the state which is not within thirty miles of a hospital. Expert bone men can be found near several of the ski areas.

The country schoolhouse

ONE GREAT PROBLEM presented to city dwellers by the conditions of country living is that of education for the children. Though the little old red schoolhouse, once inevitably fitted with the outbuilding with moon-shaped apertures, is now replaced in many towns by a modern, one-storied structure, many people may feel that what is available in such a school cannot compete with a modern city school, often the most expensive and impressive building in the neighborhood. Not merely does the country school suffer by contrast with the city counterpart as far as appearance and appointments are concerned, but the teachers, the system of teaching, and, I'm afraid it must be admitted, the quality of the scholars, are all considered to be inferior. The doctrine of the inferiority of the country school is practically nationwide; it is accepted by the city dweller, and admitted, inferentially at least, by the country man.

This universally accepted belief is not the result of a carefully worked out comparison, based upon results obtained. It is in fact the result of vigorously promoted doctrine. The hierarchy of public-school education officials throughout the land, particularly at state and national levels, have formulated a doctrine, which they are tirelessly promoting, and which includes the above as an integral part. Briefly, this doctrine accepts as truth the following postulates: That the more money spent on education, the better it is; that the more money spent for a teacher the better he is qualified to teach; that the better the physical plant the better the brand of education handed out. There is also a belief, it appears, that the observation of certain forms is more important than organization for the achievement of definite cultural or practical goals in education.

Something is amiss in both city and country schools, and it is time for a little tough-minded thinking on the subject. If the schools we think of as the best have failed miserably to educate our young people, then how bad are they? The hordes of high-school graduates who have gone into the army's special training units go in on the basis of passing merely a fourth-grade reading, writing and arithmetic examination. Our uncritical conviction that we in the United States, with our seven million young

41

people in higher educational institutions, have the best schools in the whole world must be jolted a little when we realize that the rate of illiteracy in Japan, for instance, is far lower than in the United States.

To get the answer about the quality of country schools we must question the accepted doctrine about the superiority of city schools and take a much closer look at the kinds of country schools that exist and judge them on their merits. I believe that any given school is just about as good as the community which it represents wants it to be. Whatever the faults we may find in our state-wide or nation-wide systems of education, the worth of any one given school is the reflection of the interest and will of the community or group whose children attend the school.

In all the legislatures throughout the land bills have been introduced and laws enacted to the end that rural schools be improved. All the rural organizations and all the various governmental as well as non-governmental groups interested in the conditions of country living have been urging and have kept urging that the most important single problem of rural life is the improvement of the schools. In most places most of the bills, and all of the laws and indeed all the urgings of interested groups have proposed, for the most part, one single remedy: more money.

Money is a very useful thing indeed, but there are very few problems that can be solved by money alone, and the problem of rural schools is certainly not one of them. The problem of a given rural school is the problem of the given community in which the school is located, and it can only be solved by the people who make up that community.

If you are one to whom the question of country schooling presented the greatest drawback to country living, consider these things: First, don't assume that country schools by their very nature are worse than city schools. Second, let one of the factors in deciding where in the country you are going to live be the kind of school that the given locality affords. Further, base your opinion on a careful examination of the school in question. Third, if the school is below the standards you insist on, do not let it deter you, but accept the responsibility of working in the

community and with the community to the end that the school be improved.

Remember, also, that all over the country there are enthusiastic and intelligent young people who are eager to enter the field of teaching. There is an increase of in-state and out-of-state young men and women who inquire of the school systems for teaching positions. It is reported that often they have only a bachelor's degree and no background in educational courses. This means that though they may have good credentials and be very promising as teachers in rural areas, the state—the State of Vermont, at least—is obliged to take certified people or people with some experience in teaching first. A secretary in a superintendent's office in our county found herself appalled and frustrated recently at the piles of applications that accumulated on her desk. "They seem to have the mistaken idea that *anyone* can teach," she said.

These new teachers applying for jobs in Vermont are mostly young people who want either to change their general business or the part of the country in which they live. They send applications to systems all over the state and then settle wherever they get jobs. This means that there is a lot of competition now for teaching positions at the starting salary now averaging about $6,500. Now there are only a few one-room schools left; when we came to Vermont all rural schools were of this kind.

In the year of 1929 when my wife and I were thinking of leaving the city and moving to the country, we had two children, a daughter who was in the third grade in public school and a son who was not yet old enough to attend school. Things were not ideal as far as the city school was concerned, but in spite of this the greatest single obstacle in the way of our making up our minds was the school problem. We finally came to the conclusion that we could not go on as we were, and that if we had the courage to change our way of living we surely ought to have the courage to trust our children to our own care. It seemed that they would have a finer tradition and heritage if it were one of courage and companionship; and it seemed as if, in spite of schools, the change would give them just this. As far as schooling was concerned, let come what might, we resolved that the greatest responsibility for our children's education fell upon our shoulders, more than on the schools or teachers, so that any reluctance to make the change as far as education was concerned was an admission of our own insufficiency.

We made the change. The school in the community to which we moved was a gaunt, unpainted, dilapidated structure with a tin roof, located, as a result of a bitter factional squabble in the exact geographical center of town, the worst possible place for it. I doubt if the building and location could be matched for unsuitability and bleakness by any rural school in the country. The interior was dark and dingy, the decrepit desks were battered and carved by generations of scholars, and modern facilities completely non-existent.

This was no place for our children, we decided, and as my wife happened to be a college graduate she applied for, and was granted, a teacher's certificate. By this subterfuge we could keep our child out of school, but by the same token were responsible for her formal education. Soon this procedure no longer was possible in Vermont, for the educational hierarchy so strengthened its position that no matter how well you may be equipped to teach, or how many degrees you may have, if you were not qualified in their terms by finishing a prescribed course in an accredited normal school or had not fulfilled requirements of education courses according to their standards, you could not be certified for the public-school system.

Be that as it may, we started to teach our child at home. It was not long before it was apparent that this was not going to work. There was no problem as far as learning was concerned, but the social and recreational angles of the scheme were all out of whack. Moreover, our daughter wanted to go to the school. She got to know the kids and liked them and was not happy being made a special case. Our snobbish experiment lasted about two months. After that Jane went to the country school and was much more satisfied as a result.

Now that our daughter was in school we became interested in the school, which we properly should have been in the first place. As a result of this interest my wife got herself elected to the school board at the next Town Meeting, and between us we began to think of plans to do something about the school building.

In the first place, the location was unsatisfactory; it was convenient for none of the children who attended the school. Furthermore, the small plot on which it stood could not provide for adequate play space. It seemed logical, therefore, to forget the idea of fixing up the old schoolhouse, and to look around for a better location. A school-building committee was formed with the sanction of the town at Town Meeting and the project was gotten underway.

The history of the Landgrove School Building Committee, while an interesting one, does not necessarily have a place here, nor need its achievements stand as an example for others to go by; but a brief statement of its doings might prove helpful. The place that we decided was the ideal spot with the ideal building the Farmers and Mechanics Hall, which belonged to an organization long inactive. But we were unable to procure releases from the various stockholders and at last get a deed at a nominal cost. Then we had made the first step toward a new school. The necessary funds were raised partly by soliciting contributions, but mostly by putting on dances in the Hall, to which we then had title. The Committee ran these country dances, getting the music at a nominal cost, too, and before long providing a substantial source of revenue for the school. Certain provisions of the state laws provided for state aid; and when the actual work of moving and remodeling the building was under way, a good bit of the labor, both skilled and unskilled, was furnished by the townspeople without cost. The new building was in use within a year after the project started, although it was not all paid for until some time after that.

When it was finally turned over to the town, this school had not cost the taxpayers a cent—the stipulation, by the way, which was made at Town Meeting when the town voted to let the Committee go ahead with its plans. Soon it was rated—according to the practice of the State Board of Education—as a "Superior School" because it met all the requirements then in force for a one-room school, including inside toilets, a stage, proper windows and lighting, and movable seats and desks.

So much for the physical aspects of the school and the way in which they were achieved. As for the educational achievements there over the years, the record is one to be proud of. Because this school is located in a sparsely populated mountainous township, at that time far from paved roads and electricity, there was little to offer the teacher in the way of amenities, entertainment or excitement. Yet we have been able to get some very good teachers. The pupils are few, and the maintaining of the school presents some very real problems. In fact one year the enrollment was so small that the children were transported to a neighboring town and the Landgrove school shut down.

This experiment was tried for one year and one year only, for the truth that a community gets just the kind of a school that it wants was brought forcibly home to the parents of the children. There was a noticeable change in the attitude of the children, both toward their school work and toward each other. There were fights and trouble of all sorts; and what was worse, there was a noticeable falling off in the quality of their school work. It was made obvious that if there is no connection between the community and the school, deterioration is immediately apparent.

We have been in a position to judge as to the results our school was producing, for three of our children have been through it and been graduated from the school. Besides this we have had other children at our house at one time or another who have stayed after the summer with us through the year and who have gone to this school along with our kids. These children who have come into the school from other places offer a valuable check on the relative standing of our school. In every instance the child in question has come from a city school, and in one case from formal English schools. Without exception the children have reported that they liked Landgrove's one-room country school better than any other school they have attended, and that they thought they had learned more. They all found standards up to or a little higher than those of the city schools they had left, and as far as we could find out, were more than able to hold their own when transferred to other schools later.

The English boy had been to three other schools in this country before coming to the Landgrove school. He started in the seventh grade and in one school term finished the eighth grade as well. He was outspoken in his regard for the school and frankly stated that it was the best one of the schools which he had attended in the United States, including one very good private school.

The record, which can be examined, as it pertains to the graduates of the Landgrove school, will convince anyone that it is possible to maintain a one-room rural school of high scholastic standards, even under the most adverse and primitive conditions.

The above is not an attempt to prove that all rural schools are good, or that they are better than city schools. It is merely a statement to show that good schools can be had in the country, and that any given school is very apt to be a reflection of the interest of the community—bad where there is no interest, and good where the interest is high. Basically the rural school enjoys an advantage over its city cousin, in that the classes are likely to be much smaller, and the facilities less crowded. Another thing, the one-room type of teaching, if properly conducted, has much to recommend it. It imposes more exacting demands on the teacher perhaps, but on the whole it seems to offer some advantages to the children.

The children study a good deal independently; when six or eight grades are all in one schoolroom with one teacher this is a necessity. In addition, children help each other learn, and they are free to move about and help each other when need arises. During the recess periods there is a similar freedom, and the children of different ages play together to a certain extent. Nevertheless there is also a necessary discipline to keep order in a complex situation, and the growing feeling of responsibility for order and productivity which develops when children are given a chance to go to a school of this sort.

Such small schools, if the people take an interest in them and show a willingness to put something into them, can continue to improve, even to the point where they surpass by far the large impersonal and over-crowded city schools.

The things that a child will learn in the country, and which are invaluable to him in later life, are numerous and difficult to put into words. They are things that have to do with animals and nature, and the realities of life—simple things that surround him and are a part of his daily routine, but which, living in the city, he would miss entirely. I am not making any roundabout reference to the facts of life, the birds and the bees and all that, although perhaps that is one aspect of the whole picture. Specifically I mean to refer to traits of self-reliance and self-sufficiency which country living develops in a child, to an understanding of fundamentals which the conditions of country living force upon him. No one who has ever observed a city child in the country for the first time can have any question about what I mean to convey. I am thinking of one occasion when our oldest boy, then about seven, disappeared in the forenoon, not to return until supper time, tired but full of excitement and the spirit of adventure. He had been off on his own all day, his own master, exploring at will, following trails and hunting as he went. Another time, later, when the English lad and our second son, then aged ten, went to spend the afternoon swimming at a near-by pond, they returned with a mess of frogs' legs, all dressed and ready to cook. They had caught the frogs with their bare hands and without equipment of any kind had managed to prepare them for eating. There were enough for a meal for the whole family. The first fishing of the season when a child catches his own mess of trout, the first time he is taken to track to shoot grouse, the first exploration for marsh marigolds or painted trillium and the first knowledge of the call of the hermit thrush—these all have educational value just as much as the hours spent in the classroom have, and they are experiences which are the birthright of the boy who lives in the country. They cannot be minimized or ignored, and when the question of education is evaluated they must be taken into consideration.

The child learns, moreover, which brooks have rainbow trout, and where the best holes are. He learns where the walleye lurks and how to catch a northern pike. In winter he learns how to snowshoe and ski and how to follow the tracks of animals in the snow, and in the woods in any season he discovers the related ways of animals and insects and birds and where the plant foods grow that sustain a great many of those creatures. Children today are even learning how to detect edible wild foods and how to make camp and live in the wilderness.

In the matter of schools, there is, to my mind, a horrendous trend in these times toward consolidation at all levels—this in spite of the fact that the most recent evidence seems to indicate that primary education is best achieved in small, local schools where several grades are conducted within the same class.

In other words, the small, one- or two-room schools where the kids walked to class did a better job in the past than the huge, gadgeted, expensive, brick and glass institutions which are now erupting all over the rural countryside.

My advice—and I speak from experience—is not to be discouraged if you discover the location you have selected offers naught but the old-fashioned, rural grade school. Secondary schools are another story, and there are few places in Vermont where access to a good, modern high school is not now available.

In short, if parents have the guts and the interest and are willing to assume a good part of the responsibility themselves, the best place for the education of children, impressive and highly-equipped edifices to the contrary not withstanding, is in the country.

Selecting a place to live & what to look for

When the Roman poet Horace expressed what he wanted to own, he said "a piece of land not so very large, and near the house an ever-flowing spring of water, and above this a bit of woodland." Foresters and farmers want to own productive land, good for the crops of trees, for the grain and garden produce they want to grow or rich with pastures and cornfields for the stock they want to raise. Though they admire these qualities of land, many people deciding to move to the country in these days are actually wanting solitude, seclusion, cleaner air, altitude or perhaps a fine view with a trout brook thrown in; these other benefits are pure gravy.

People want a simpler life. Now that each part of the world is rapidly accessible from any other part and nations and communities are no longer isolated from each other, the new sense of time and place has changed our view of life and our values. Our imaginations are fired and our enthusiasm is excited by all this change. At least so we think and talk and dream. But when it comes to doing, there is plenty of evidence that we don't actually like the world we live in. The concentration of population, the increased tempo of living resulting from both the speed of our travel and the more and more complete mechanization all around us have produced extraordinary dissatisfactions in many people.

The established lawyer with a practice in the city after returning from a mountain-climbing trip with his family finds himself hating the thought of returning to the metropolitan existence. Country dwellers who have taken jobs in defense plants in the cities flock back to the country either in the state they came from or in a new country location in the south or in the west. People exhausted by traffic, noise, air pollution and the endless crowds on city streets give it all up and go up from Los Angeles into the mountain, out from Houston to a ranch, away from Chicago or Washington or New York to a farming country where they can breathe again and leave behind the ills and pressures of city life.

Actually for the person who plans to buy country property and settle down the first consideration is "What will it cost?" Unless you are lucky enough to find a place remote from **any** of the areas people choose for recreation or land speculation, you will find that the price you have to pay is influenced by these two factors.

Where there are mountains and snow, as in Vermont, there has been an influx of vacationers, of motel and lodge keepers to house them, and of land developers to buy up land and sell them lots. Where there is water, summer visitors and owners of boats have influenced land values and prices. In many places there seems to be a rather ominous advance along this front. In various states, including Vermont, there have been far-sighted environmental protection laws passed and local zoning established which have made land speculation a little less attractive than it was when the quick-buck fellows had it all their own way without any controls. My suggestions, therefore, to anyone taking the step of moving to the country these days is to steer clear of the vacation spots and the areas that attract the developers.

One of your main reasons in moving to the country is to put down your roots in a community, preferably one that is stable and long-lived, not a transient clustering of week-end chalets or a modern condominium built like a city apartment house, but located on the side of a mountain or at the end of a lake.

Find a town that has a history and a well-rooted life of its own. Find several, if possible, and write to the Town Clerks of each to get answers to your basic questions about what it costs to live in that town. Ask what the tax rate is, and the proportion of the market value charged to the taxpayer in establishing this rate. Ask the number of properties for sale in the town, and the prices that are being asked. Ask about the schools, both elementary and secondary and about any junior college there may be, or plans for one. Request that a Town Report be sent to you, if that is possible.

I think it is sensible, furthermore, to inquire into the local public utility rates—usually, as far as I know, too high to make heating with electricity other than relatively expensive. And ask about rate raises, for the utilities

have been asking for raises several times a year recently. Where there is natural gas available, ask about that also. If you are moving to a climate where there is snow, you have to remember that heavy, wet snow and the formation of ice can break electric lines and give the householder who depends on electricity a bad time. My son heats with a gas furnace and wood burning and does not find that it is extravagant. We heat with fuel oil (having converted from wood,) and this is a bit less expensive. It is my impression that electric heat for year-round use is an expensive proposition.

If you have not already concluded your plans for moving to the country and already bought your place, here are the steps to take to avoid later distress or trouble:

1. Make sure the title of your intended property is clear. The small fee an attorney will charge to search the title may save trouble later and may uncover some interesting historical lore about your place as a special dividend. If you are taking out a mortgage, you will be required to have a title search.

2. Talk with the town selectmen or road commissioner and find out whether your intended home is on a town-maintained road or better. If it isn't, give weight to what this may mean to you after the Spring rains. If you have any thought of winter residence, find out, too, if the roads are regularly plowed.

3. When your property title is searched, look for clauses that might give a neighbor a right-of-way through that plot your wife plans for an old-fashioned rose garden. See, too, that someone else doesn't own the water rights to your bubbling spring. If your water supply is on someone else's property, investigate that, too, to see if your rights to it are binding.

4. Investigate the assessment now on your intended property and if you buy be sure no back taxes are owed. Find out the tax rate of your town and the usual basis of evaluation. Estimate how your intended improvements to the property will affect your annual tax bill.

You may encounter expenses in making your house airtight, and installing adequate water, and sewage disposal. Whether you are going to buy an old house or build a new one, it is imperative that dwellings, especially in the northern states, be made as airtight as possible. The use of insulation is a must in these times when every room in the house is heated. In olden days, when only the kitchen and livingroom were heated, the pot-bellied wood stoves could keep one warm, if one stayed close enough. Feather puffs sufficed in the bedrooms.

In deciding about a house, you should select one that is protected from the prevailing winds, with the exposure such that there is plenty of sun. Old-time builders often selected the sites for their building operations with a nice eye as to livability, but they all did not always hit it right; it will pay to check. Care at this stage of the game will pay dividends in fuel saved in winter and in daily pleasure and comfort. To have a house in a snug and cozy spot open to the sun and sheltered from the winds is of more importance than a breath-taking view.

Whenever possible, in remodeling an old house, it will pay to do all possible within the scope of your pocketbook to keep in the heat and keep out the cold in the north or keep in the coolness and keep out the heat in warm climates in the south or west. Interwall and overhead insulation is a fairly expensive proposition, however, and its cost may make it prohibitive. The generous use of inexpensive building paper, and of insulating wall boards, if properly installed, will go far towards making a house tight without the use of expensive inter-wall insulation. I have remodeled several barns for use as dwellings and wherever possible the old barn siding was taken off, paper applied to the liners, and then the outside boards replaced. Inside, the studs were covered with cheap $1/2$ inch lumber put on horizontally, then covered with paper, and the interior finish of planed pine or spruce boards laid vertically on top of the paper was applied. The resultant cross section of the outside wall was board, paper, board, air space, board, paper, board, and the efficiency of this wall as an insulator has been demonstrated beyond question of doubt.

Water is not supplied by water companies in the rural areas, nor is sewage disposed of by discharge into a municipal sewer. Thus both of these requirements must be assessed before any final commitment is made. If you neglect sensible consideration of these things, you may discover impossible conditions when it is too late.

Rural water supplies come either from wells or springs. The wells can be stone-lined holes in the ground reaching down to ground water (which may be from ten to thirty feet below the surface.) But these sources of supply, except in rare instances, will be found inadequate. For here as everywhere else, the level of the water table is dropping, and the seepage into shallow wells is too slow to supply water for the uses to which we all have become accustomed: flush toilets, washing machines, daily hot showers, etc.

The other kind is the driven well, where a machine drills a five- or six-inch hole into the ground close by the house, the metal casing descending as the hole deepens. These wells often are referred to erroneously as "Artesian," for unless the water in the casing rises to or above the surface, the well is not truly "Artesian." Such wells in Vermont are as scarce as piebald chickadees.

Thus most driven wells have to have a pump to bring the water up and provide pressure, and that pump must be driven by electricity.

The cost of drilling these wells varies slightly from area to area, but it amounts roughly to eight dollars a foot. The drill man will tell you what flow per minute you require, and if he is honest he will stop drilling when this flow is achieved. The cost of the pump is extra, and from local experience I should say the average cost of a driven well is about $1,500. But beware of geological pitfalls. Inquire about the depth of wells in your immediate neighborhood, for the cost depends on how deep the driller has to go to find an adequate vein of water.

Spring water is the ideal supply, particularly if the source is higher than the highest intended point of discharge and the spring's flow is always adequate.

However, there is a dark side to this lovely, bucolic picture of having your own spring. Springs, more often than not, are contaminated by the seepage of surface water, and all must be tested for purity before they can be safely used.

If a proper source of water can be found with sufficient head to supply the building with fair pressure, this makes the ideal water system. A gravity system should avoid syphons or low spots in the line if it is at all possible to do so, for once a syphon is lost it may require considerable trouble to restore it, and under certain conditions low spots or sags will collect air pockets which will effectively stop the flow of water. In cold climates take precautions that the line is installed so that there is a minimum danger from freezing. Often it is impractical, because of expense, to lay the pipe deeper below the surface than the frost can possibly penetrate. If the line is susceptible to freezing see that the plumbing is so arranged that in winter the water in the outside pipes may be kept constantly running, and remember that any stoppage in the flow of the water may have very serious results indeed. Once a water line is frozen it is a tough job to thaw it out, and when thawed you will probably discover that the pipe has been burst by the irresistible force of the expanding ice. There are several ways in which a frozen pipe may be thawed, by electricity, by thaw tubes, or by application of heat directly to the frozen section. Any one of these methods is an expensive nuisance, and in spite of all efforts, sometimes a frozen line will remain frozen until spring when nature will take care of it. Believe me, I speak feelingly and with knowledge on the subject. The best and only thing is to be sure that the line is not going to freeze.

When a gravity supply is out of the question, pressure for the water system must be supplied by a pump, which will either lift the water to a gravity tank, or force it into a pressure tank. These pumps are either manually or power operated. It is a considerable chore to maintain sufficient pressure by hand, and while it is the least expensive system, I would not advise its use.

In places where electricity is not available a very satisfactory pressure system can be installed, the power for which is supplied by an air-cooled gasoline-powered engine. These systems are not expensive, and they have an automatic cut-off. They must be started by hand and failure of the motor or difficulty in starting can cause considerable inconvenience. In some instances the force of the wind may be used to pump the water into a storage tank. Pressure tank systems are more satisfactory than gravity tanks, and in cold regions the gravity tank system is not very practical. There is, of course, the ancient system of collecting the rain water from the roofs by means of cisterns. The water collected is beautifully soft, and in regions where, due to geological formations, all ground water is hard, such a system has much to recommend it as an auxiliary source of supply. It is not, however, suitable for drinking purposes unless treated.

If stream water is used and there is sufficient flow of water available, a hydraulic ram can be installed. The hydraulic ram is one of the most ingenious and, at the same time, one of the simplest devices ever produced by man, and I have often wondered why it was not more widely used. The momentum of the flowing water is used to generate pressure, and it is completely automatic in operation, albeit somewhat noisy.

Whether you are young or old, and are moving to the country for a new life for your family or a new life of retirement, when you find the place you want and make arrangements to buy it, you face all the problems of being transplanted. Transplanting is an operation that has its dangers as anyone who works with flowers or shrubs knows. Each spring I set out little plants for whole days at a time, taking them out of their secure places in the coldframe, sticking them into alien ground of the garden where there is no protection, and where certainly some will never take root and thus die. If the weather is right that day, I can expect the hundreds of leeks and celeriac I set out to thrive, and I know that most will survive. And people will survive transplanting, too, but he who undertakes to start his roots in strange soil would be well advised to know all he can about all that is involved both in the practical, basic matters already discussed and in matters concerning particulars of the land and house, too.

When you move from a city apartment to a place of your own in the country, you no longer have a landlord; you are a steward of your land.

You will want to confer with the representatives of your Natural Resources District—the new name for the Soil Conservation District. They can provide invaluable technical assistance on projects you might undertake (installing a pond, using some of the land for grazing) as well as information on what have been past uses of your property. Their office has the results of previous Tests of your soil on record; you can learn about its mineral richness, acidity or alkalinity, and you might be pleasantly surprised by the qualities of soil they reveal.

The staff will provide information concerning landowner services, and you will find that they adhere to a responsibility to the community and environmental balance as well. They will help you make your first important decisions, and develop a conservation plan which concerns the uses you wish to make of your property. The staff's services are available at any time you may need further assistance.

You can also find men to help you find out about forest management, the use of your land for stock, and the expenses you will have for additional water if needed. Check on the wells, springs, streams and pond water available, for you will be less than happy if you are going to have to put up with water shortages.

The other side of the water problem is sewage. Direct discharge into any stream is forbidden by law, so this simple expedient of the oldtimers is denied us—and a good thing, too. The answer is the installation of an adequate 500 gallon or larger septic tank, complete with a drainage field, properly laid out so that all the effluent is eventually absorbed in the ground.

I can't give you exact figures, but you had better be prepared to sink at least a thousand dollars in this project, along with the tank, unless you find sandy and gravelly soil to discharge into. These points all must be looked into before your final decision is made. (Vermont's Law 250 now offers strict regulations in these matters.)

Septic tanks may be bought made of sheet metal or of glazed tile, the latter of which are the more expensive, or, one may be built, cast in place of concrete, with proper baffle plates set in the masonry. Care should be used to see that, whatever the type of tank, it be properly installed. In the first place, keep the drain from the kitchen sink from discharging into the septic tank, if this is possible. If it is not possible it is wise to install a grease trap, as grease and too much soap slow up the bacteriological action of the tank. Another thing, see that the capacity of the tank is adequate for current use and for all probable increase in use as well.

If the soil is too shallow or water-logged, if the ledges are too close to the surface, if the seepage could block up or get into someone else's (or your own) water system, you do not have an appropriate location for a septic tank.

In most states having environmental laws applications for any private sewage system must include certified reports from a sanitary engineer including records of the highest known surface water elevations for the last ten years, evidence of any nearby sources of drinking water, and a statement from the engineer that the proposals for your septic tank are in accord with state and town health regulations.

These are considerations you must be prepared to face in any part of the country, in farm areas, villages, or forest areas recently coming into residential use.

If your search for a country place leads you really far out and way back, there are some other considerations to be studied. If your place is beyond the present power lines, be sure to ascertain how much it is going to cost to have these lines extended. This is not now the problem that it was in the days when the Ogdens came to Vermont. Our initial inquiries made it clear that we could not possibly meet the requirements of the power company. For about the first twenty years of our residence here, therefore, we got along without electricity. And I must say that we got along very well indeed.

Electricity is the handmaiden of modern technology, whose inexorable advance is really terrifying. Once you have the use of electricity you cannot get along without it. The memory of happy, less frenetic days B.E. is lost before you whip up the first soufflé in the electric blender.

The proliferation of electrically-operated gadgets shows no sign of abating. Until it does, there is not much sense in getting upset about the deterioration of our environment. The demand for electric power is the devil in the machine. The depletion of our natural resources and the fouling of our environment springs from this most important single source.

It is futile to talk of control unless this point is recognized. Here in Vermont the answer to increased demand for electricity seems to be atomic power plants, and on this controversial subject all the facts are not in.

One other aspect to being far in and way out cannot be overlooked. This is the matter of accessibility.

The place you have lost your heart to was once occupied by a family whose means of transportation required no more than a narrow road winding its way between high banks, belly deep in snow in Winter and knee deep in mud in the Spring. In Summer the dust was taken for granted.

So, dear friend, take heed of this point. You may be able to get by with some sort of four-wheel drive vehicle, but this means you will want some other form of transportation garaged out on the blacktop. Not only will you have your moments of despair, but the town fathers will find it impossible to supply the services you demand.

Once long ago a man and wife came to this town, and they found their hearts' desire in just such a place as I have described. The first Winter produced a crisis of major proportions. As a selectman, I could not see it possible to supply them a road for automobile traffic, and here I came face to face with bitterness and hatred I had not experienced before in all my life.

During the first Winter these people gave up. Even later, in the

Summertime, they found the isolation and loneliness unendurable, and so they sold the place. As of now a nice family with sporting blood, young muscles and a Jeep are making some sort of a go of it during their Winter vacations. The town now has more money, and the road has been improved. But still this place is not suitable for year-round occupancy.

When we found our place in the country and decided on the house where we wanted to live, we were prepared to do the necessary work to make this house habitable the year round. As with everyone else, we recognized that the house with its land is the first practical problem. But it is important when considering this problem to remember that the principal occupations of the owners are of prime significance and that they shape many decisions. If the house is to be a farm house, and the principal occupation of the owner farming, entirely different conditions govern the selection of a place from those when the place is to be merely a dwelling in the country, whether for weekends, vacations or year round. Success in farming certainly depends on having a good farm, with soil and climate adapted to the successful growing of the crops he has in mind to produce and the cattle he intends to raise. Often personal and sentimental reasons enter into the decision as well, and in many instances chance plays a part and actually exercises the final decision in the selection of a new home place.

Throughout the nation there are beautiful rural areas that have been attractive to vacationers since the beginning of the century. Some fade in popularity and some come back into favor. Many a man has remembered his youthful summertime experiences in a country refuge for a whole lifetime, and has felt the urge to move back.

To my personal knowledge and experience Vermont has been a refuge and a haven for out-of-state people from as far back as 1905. Before then the mountains and the spas and lakes of Vermont, along with similar places all over New England, were considered suitable for vacation interludes.

So in the summertime the steam trains carried many people northward, where they found their ways from the ornate railroad depots to either fashionable hotels or to humble boarding places, in grateful escape from the cities.

But I am not speaking of these people, nor of the fancy and rambling hotels, nor of the carriage trails up the mountainsides, nor of the healing waters of Vermont's many medicinal springs. Even at the turn of the century the springs were beginning to be choked and the frame monstrosities, many the victims of fire, were disappearing. No longer were most of the carriage roads more than trails for hikers and runways for the denizens of the forest.

Starting at least sixty years ago, and probably first in the place where I am most familiar (in the uplands of Bennington County), out-of-state people were buying the abandoned farms, along with their still-sound and liveable farmhouses, which could be had for a song.

Here was something entirely new. These people were not itinerant vacationists or peripatetic health-seekers; they were different, for they became property owners. Immediately they contributed to the economy of the community, for besides paying taxes in increasing amounts, they spent money on reconstruction, for general labor and with the local merchants.

Of course, there were a scattering few throughout the state who earlier went away, and, having made their piles, came back to their native town or village, where they bought property. But I am not talking about these rare enough native sons. In the beginning *my people* had not even heard of Vermont. This is what happened:

One Sunday morning in the Spring of 1903 Mr. and Mrs. David C. Grant stood in the sunshine on the steps of the Westminster Presbyterian Church in Elizabeth, N.J. and talked animatedly with a young man who had just finished his stint in the pulpit as guest preacher. He spoke with poetic abandon of the hills and countryside of Vermont, and of the tiny village in which he had been born. His descriptions of the scene were so entrancing and the story of abandonment so convincing that Mr. Grant felt that in this place one might find everything that the soul could ask for in the way of physical setting, and at the same time some rare bargains in real estate.

His impression was so vivid that he set out on a journey of exploration, and he took along another Elizabethan. In their quest for the promised land in Peru they descended from the Green Mountain Flyer at Manchester, where they soon located the stage which crossed the mountain over the old toll road. Eventually they came to the tiny village of Peru, which lay high on the southeast slope of Bromley Mountain in the midst of a lovely rural setting.

Looking over this beautiful countryside they must have felt as Keats described his feelings upon his first look into a copy of Chapman's *Homer.* And these two cultivated and enterprising gentlemen, along with their charming wives, were just the right people arriving in the right place at exactly the right time. Soon through their influence commenced the rehabilitation of Peru, and eventually also of a good bit of rural Vermont.

And that is one version, at any rate, of how it started.

The house in which we have lived for the past forty years seems, looking back upon the events, to have been thrust upon us by fate. True we were not seriously interested in farming, nor were we even sure we were going to live out in the country. Having made the decision at Slide Mountain to leave the metropolitan area, we decided it would be worthwhile to take the time to scout around a bit, and look over certain sections of the country accessible by car to our home in New Jersey. Our travels carried as far south and west as Kentucky, with stops in Maryland and Virginia, and through Pennsylvania and New York into Vermont where we stopped to see friends for a visit one October.

While there we learned that in a certain small country store in a remote settlement, extra fine cheeses were to be found. Our host, who considered himself a connoisseur of cheeses, found in John Colburn, the proprietor of this store, a kindred spirit, and he felt that only here in this store could he be sure of buying a good cheese. My wife and I felt that we would like to take a ride through the back roads of the Green Mountains at the time our host set out to get his cheese, so we decided to go along with him.

As we approached our destination we came to a ramshackle farm house which our host said was for sale and which could be bought very reasonably. We stopped the car and looked through the windows at dismal and poverty-stricken squalor within; we saw the tumble-down wood shed, the crumbling chimney, the briar choked door yard, the untended fields, and the glorious view of valley and mountains beyond. We then proceeded less than a mile further and came to the village where John Colburn kept his store.

The village was a deserted one and a more dismal broken-down deserted village would be impossible to imagine. John Colburn and his brother were the only inhabitants. Here at the store while we looked over and bought the cheese, the story of the village was told. During John Colburn's account he mentioned that most if not all of the places were for sale and the prices asked for the various places were extremely reasonable. There in the store was born the idea of purchasing all the properties, including the first one we looked at and of rehabilitating the village. It took us some time and a good deal of arranging, but eventually just this was accomplished. The house we chose out of the eight in the village, while one of the most decrepit, we decided on because of its lines and livability. Questions of climate or farm facilities or tillage were not considered, because at the time the decision was made to take over the village, we had no idea that living there would turn out to be a permanent arrangement. When the depression came, the question was decided for us, however, and we have never regretted these decisions.

The above example is cited to show that oftimes fate does take a hand in deciding questions which, theoretically at least, should be decided in other ways.

In all, I have rebuilt as many as 40 old houses, quite a few of them in the last stages of disrepair, and for those who are deciding whether to restore an old house or begin with a new building, I say it is more economical to fix up an old house than it is to start from scratch and build a new one. I assume, of course, that the cubage and facilities are to be the same in the old and new. And I know that not all will agree with me for many carpenters and workmen dislike to work on old houses because nothing is ever plumb or true, nothing is new and clean, and much of the work is dirty and puttering. Consider however, that when you start with an old frame, even though everything that meets the eye upon completion may be new—new roof, new siding, new sash, new floors, new plumbing and all—you have not had to excavate, nor grade, nor plant, nor build the frame, including rafters and roof boards.

When looking over the house, observe certain things. If it is a frame house—as most old houses are—it is probably built with heavy timbers for sills, and plates and posts. This kind of house can get into pretty bad shape before it need be discarded. The framing in this structure starts with heavy sills, generally eight by eight inches, with the floor area divided so that all the bearing partitions that support the second story rest on heavy sleepers, also eight by eight inches. These sleepers are framed into the sills and carry the floor joists. The sleepers are generally so placed that in no instance do the floor joists carry a long span. In many old houses. these joists are farther apart than in modern construction and may consist of logs hewn flat on the upper side. This type of construction results in a certain amount of spring in the floor which is not necessarily a sign of structural weakness in the floor itself. In fact if the sleepers and sills are sound the joists can be replaced, or new joists can be put in between the existing old joists. See that the posts at the four corners are sound and also the second floor sleepers framed in to correspond with the sleepers on the first floor. All heavy timbers should be well tied to the posts with mortised braces. In a well-built old house the plates as well are of heavy timbers and are carried by posts so that the studs in the outside walls and in the partitions have very little if any structural responsibility. In a house framed in this manner almost any partition may be removed without damaging the strength of the floors or the structure of the house.

Such a building will stand a good bit of racking, in fact it may be likened to a well-built crate or packing box, which may be rolled down a steep hill and arrive at the bottom without serious damage. One instance comes to mind where the dry stone foundation wall in a timber framed house had fallen away, leaving the sill supported on each end only. This condition had existed for so long a time that the sill sagged with the weight of the building so that the middle of the timber was three inches lower than the ends. When jack screws were placed under the low part of the sill with the idea of straightening it, it was discovered that the bend had been in the stick for so long a time, and the framing of the house had become so adjusted to it that upon raising the center, the building was lifted from the foundation at each end as well. With this type of framing rotten pieces may be cut out of the sills or plates and new pieces spliced in. Posts and plates may be repaired as well.

The place to look for trouble is first of all in the cellar. In climates where, because of cold winters, the houses were banked, one is likely to find sill trouble. Some of the old timers evidently figured that if they took the banking away in the spring, they only had to put it back again in the fall, so why go to all that bother. Consequently they left their houses banked all year around, renewing the banking from time to time, be it sods or sawdust or leaves, or even manure, as they saw fit. The result of holding moisture against the lower part of the building and keeping the air away from it as this procedure was bound to do, was that the sills and the lower part of the studs and posts rotted. Check from the cellar side by jabbing a sharp case knife into the wood of the sill. If the wood is soft and punky to the depth of greater than two or three inches the timber is in need of replacement, or repair. Check from the outside as well, if this is possible. If there is any suspicion of rot in the sills it will pay to remove the splash boards and liners and check on conditions from the outside as well as from the in.

It will be impossible to foresee all the conditions which will develop in fixing over an old house, but it will pay to make reasonable effort to find out as much as you possibly can. In a timber framed house, entire sills, or portions of sills can be replaced without extravagant cost, and studs which are not structurally important can be spliced by merely laying in a short piece of two-by-four long enough to reach from the sound portion of the stud to the sill, and spiking it firmly in place. Check next on the sleepers and floor joists. If the sleepers are sound, old floors can be strengthened by scabbing a piece of two by four on to the sleepers and inserting new joists between the old ones. If the sleepers are gone beyond repair it is a more serious problem. Provided there is sufficient head room, jury sleepers can be rigged under the old ones, supported by posts. If this procedure is adopted be sure that the posts are on sound footing and are well up out of any possible moisture.

The next place to look for trouble is in the attic, where neglect of the roof may have permitted water to enter and rot the plates and the upper ends of the posts. The rafters should likewise be examined for possibility of rot. Posts, plates, and rafters can, however, be repaired, even if the damage appears to be quite extensive.

It is welcome news to some newcomers to find that in this type of frame house the foundations are not important, or at least not as structurally important as they are in the balloon type of framing. From the point of view of comfort and cleanliness, however, and freedom from rodents, sound cellar walls laid up in masonry and mortar are well worth having. Nevertheless, one can get along without a good cellar, and without square and secure cellar walls; in fact we have done just that for years in this house, but to live without them is to appreciate them all the more.

The next place to look for trouble—and if it's an old house, you are almost sure to find it—is in the chimneys. Chimneys are the one part of the house where it will not pay to temporize. Many of the old chimneys were built only one course of brick thick, and none of them were lined with flue tile. Every chimney not lined is a very potent fire hazard. It will not pay to fool with an old chimney. Time and expense and peace of mind will be saved if all questionable or unlined chimneys are torn down and rebuilt at the very beginning. If it is necessary to tear down and rebuild a chimney, use plenty of care and thought in deciding where and how it is to be rebuilt. Get all the flues you can into one chimney. If you have to rebuild a chimney consider including a fireplace, for while a fireplace is an inefficient heating unit, to be sure, it is not a great added expense to the building of a chimney and adds so much in pleasure and good cheer, and even in comfort, that it is worth thinking about. Try to arrange the location of the chimney so that not only will it serve the furnace and include a fireplace but that it may carry the flue for the kitchen stove as well.

If you discover that the cost of tearing out the old and installing a new chimney, including the fireplaces which you would like to have, is going to be more expensive than you can afford, do not become discouraged and give up the idea entirely. Professional masons are expensive, and there is a deal of mumbo-jumbo currently regarding the building of fireplaces, but actually the materials involved cost relatively little and the rules for building a fireplace are simple. I am not rash enough to state that anyone can build a fireplace and chimney, but a person who is not afraid of hard work, who has some gift for working with his hands, and who can get some competent unskilled help, certainly can do it, and save himself a considerable sum of money by so doing.

When we started to fix over the old farmhouse in which we are now living we discovered that not only were the chimneys constructed of a single course and unlined, but that they were suspended chimneys as well. That is, they had no bearing on any foundation of any sort whatsoever, but were built on plank platforms which were supported by the second floor beams. Moreover, the house, which had been built around 1840, about the time that Ben Franklin's stoves were coming into the ripeness of their maturity, had no fireplaces in it. So it was decided that the existing chimneys should be torn down, and two new chimneys built. One in the north end of the house to carry a flue for the wood-burning furnace which we planned to install, and also to include a fireplace in our living room.

The other, more centrally located to carry the kitchen stove flue, and to include a big fireplace in the other living room or den in the south end of the house. As I laid the plans which I had sketched before each contractor in succession, I was confronted with estimates of cost which not only seemed to me to be out of reason, but definitely beyond the scope of our means. I had heard of a friend of a friend of ours who had built himself a chimney and fireplace in a hunting camp of his, and I decided if he could do it, I could too. The next week was spent in a critical study of all the fireplaces in the neighborhood that I was able to stick my head inside of. Conclusions gleaned from these observations, and a few basic principles imparted to me by an architect friend, plus the adventurous spirit of one of my neighbor helpers who had never built a chimney, gave me the courage to start. The two chimneys were built at last, without too much trouble and at a surprisingly low cost, and they have been successfully operating ever since that day, now over 40 years ago. Since those first two, I have built many more all over this part of Vermont, many in stone, some in brick and even some in cement blocks. Outside of the physical labor involved and the wear and tear on the skin of one's hands there is nothing to deter the moderately hardy person from building a simple fireplace and chimney. Corbelled hearths, multiple flues, and upstairs fireplaces can become complicated, it is true, but a few simple ones successfully built will give the courage to tackle even more complicated structures.

The open fire indoors ranks high as a solace to the spirit of man wherever, in winter, the days are cold and nights long. As a means of heating an enclosed space or preparing a meal, the fireplace has been long since surpassed by various modern devices, and the use of wood for fuel in this country, even in places where it is plentiful is very expensive. Nevertheless, some atavistic instinct remains a part of us so that for young and old a fire of burning logs exerts a fascination and satisfies a need which cannot be denied.

Up until a century and a half ago the elegance of any newly built house was measured by the number of its fireplaces, just as now it is measured by the number of its bathrooms; then Dr. Franklin came along with his notion for enclosing the fire with the walls of iron. Almost overnight the practical overcame the aesthetic, and fireplaces, expensive to build and inefficient to operate, were no longer used. Before long central heating outmoded Dr. Franklin's parlor stoves, leaving only the range in the kitchen where a wood fire might still be seen to burn.

Along with the changing methods new fuels came into use so that today, with automatic furnaces fired by either gas or oil in the utility compartment and electric ranges in the kitchen, there no longer remains any need for wood fires in our homes. But we have discovered that our desire remains, and old houses with open fireplaces are in high demand. Mantle pieces which surround blank plaster are being pounced upon as perhaps concealing a sealed opening, and all new dwellings, be they ranch type or Cape Cod, come equipped with a place for an open fire, in one form or another. Only in city apartments or in the low-cost suburban housing development is there no place to sit and dream as the flaming wood crumbles into coals and the smoke drifts upward. To sit and dream, that is, if one has the wood to burn!

When we came to the country to live nearly forty years ago there were no fuels available except wood and kerosene. Without electricity, oil-burning furnaces were out of the question even if the furnace oil had been made available, and many miles of mountain roads precluded the use of coal for heating the house. So we used wood: great two- and three-foot chunks in the furnace, four-foot cord wood in one fireplace, and stove wood in the kitchen to cook with. I got to learn quite a bit about wood as fuel, an education which had begun long ago on my grandfather's farm in Dyberry, Pennsylvania.

There was no fireplace in this house and in winter, besides the kitchen stove, which was, if I remember right, a Home Comfort, there were two wood-burning heaters. One was an air-tight sheet metal chunk stove in the dining room which was fed from the top, its maw capable of swallowing 40-pound chunks of bone dry rock maple at one gulp, and these would keep going all night long. The other, in the living room (the parlor also had a stove, but this room was not kept open in winter) was a tall majestic affair crowned with a shiny nickel-trimmed cover which opened onto a water compartment, whose great cast iron girth was pierced with many a mica window so that, after the lights were out, cheerful shadows would dance on the walls and ceiling as the red flames flickered within. Oh! It was an imposing piece of machinery, and the very deuce of a job to take down when summer came, but it was not as good a keeper as the chunk stove in the dining room, and many a winter morning Uncle Will came down in his stockinged feet to find that his fire had gone out.

It was my chore to keep the woodbin filled for Aunt Fanny while I was at my uncle's farm on summer vacations. One time I piled the wood in my arms so high that I could barely see over the top, and as a result I stumbled coming through the kitchen door. Grandfather was seated by the kitchen table, and once the clatter died away he said: "Take care, boy, take care! That comes from carrying a lazy-man's load." I have carried those words in my memory ever since.

Most of my uncle's wood came from a lot several miles away which had been cut over for timber a generation before. Most of what we brought down consisted of 12- to 16-foot poles not over six inches or so at the butt. This was not the best for winter fires, but it served very well for the summer kitchen. It consisted of black and pin cherry, ironwood, hard and red maple, black and yellow birch, and even poplar and alder.

These poles were sawed into billets about 16 inches long on a saw rig with a heavy flywheel and tilting table, which was set up in the chip-yard in front of the shop, connected by a 12-foot belt with the one-cylinder gasoline engine within. The winter fuel came from body wood, preferably of beech, birch or maple, sawed into 4-foot lengths right where the tree had been felled, by means of a shad-bellied two-man saw.

These great chunks were then split and stacked in the woods, to be brought home later on when the sledding was good.

Though today it is possible to use power saws and draw out the wood behind a tractor or jeep, each of the operations in the old days—chopping, sawing and splitting—while the most arduous kind of labor, were somehow soul-satisfying as well as muscle-building. To have the sharp bit of the axe slap into the tree exactly where directed, to see the good-sized chips fly out, to sever the limbs with one powerful stroke close to the trunk—all afford substantial satisfaction. And the rhythm of sawing! Each body swinging in perfect synchronization, pulling, never pushing, straight strokes never bending the saw blade, all the while bearing down sparingly so as to get the most cut from the least effort—these too afford real pleasure. The saw, nevertheless, played as great a part as did the sawyers, for if the cutting teeth were not sharply filed and set, and if the rakers were not of the proper length, the long, thick curling worms of wood would not follow the stroke, and the saw would bind and balk to the complete frustration of the sawyers despite their efforts.

Splitting was the hardest work of all, but here too there were satisfactions. True, in tight-grained, frozen chunks of green wood it is almost impossible to get the wedge started, for after scoring with the axe in a likely spot on the end grain, and gently tapping the bit of the wedge into the mark so that it would stand unsupported, the first heavy blow only served to cause the wedge to jump out again as if one were attempting to split rubber. And ancient yellow birch butts are so stringy and their fibers so intertwined and twisted that they simply refuse to split. One can sweat and swear over a stringy piece like that for as much time as it would take to split a quarter of a cord of clean-grained beech or maple. With clean-grained wood it is music to the ears to hear the pop of the stick as it is riven by one or two expert blows.

I learned a good bit about trees and their products in those early days, for Uncle Will was both interested and well informed, and he happily taught me all he knew. Long ago, before anyone ever heard of "ecology," Uncle

Will knew what it meant. He pointed out to me various associations between plants and trees and animals which were fascinating to observe, and useful to know about.

I learned that ironwood (hop-hornbeam) was the hardest and toughest of all woods native to that place, and that it was the best wood to use for a wagon reach; that hemlock would resist rot above ground, but that it was shaky and not strong for construction uses; that hickory made the best tool handles and axe helves; that in building, spruce was used for structural members, and white pine for trim; locust and cedar for fence posts; white ash for fork and hoe handles; beech, oak and maple for flooring, black cherry and walnut for cabinetry; beech for brush backs and handles; willow for gunpowder charcoal; elm for barrels; basswood for butter tubs; and so forth, etc.

At an early age I was able to recognize all the native trees. Having been trained to notice, I located exotic species which some freak of fate or the hand of man had placed in strange surroundings, and I spotted unusual specimens among the natives. I knew that all softwoods were not soft and that all hardwoods were not hard, that one evergreen (tamarack) lost its leaves in the fall, and that one good-sized shrub (witch hazel) blossomed in the fall, not in the spring. I learned that moss does not necessarily grow on the north side of a tree trunk, but that the shape of a tree in an exposed place will tell the direction of the prevailing wind. I learned many things about the forests and the trees, how to recognize a tree by its shape and bark when the leaves were off, and how to spot the different varieties of wood by their grain.

If you are unfamiliar with the uses of fireplace wood, here are a few basic considerations. First of all, the measure of quantity is bulk not weight, and the unit is a cord. In a way this is unfortunate, because in general the weight of dry wood is the measure of its usefulness as fuel. Moreover a cord can mean different things to different people, nor is it always what it seems. I had an old woodsman come to me one winter during the depression, and he offered to put up cordwood out of down hardwood tops for a dollar a cord. Well, a cord measures 8 feet long, 4 feet deep and 4 feet high, 128 cubic feet in all, and that seemed like a lot of wood for an old man to put up for a dollar. With qualms of conscience I told him to go ahead, but after I had examined his first day's wood pile I felt less guilty of economic exploitation, for as the saying goes around here, "You could throw a cat right through it anywhere."

Besides artful piling, watch out for useless or rotten wood. If you buy cordwood green, let it season for at least the months of the summer solstice before you use it. In those days I also learned that green wood would burn all right, but it was difficult to ignite. Once it got going it seemed to make a hotter fire than dry wood but it did not last as long, and worst of all, it produced great quantities of creosote, a sticky liquid smelling like carbolic acid which stained walls and dripped on rugs and hardened into a combustible coke which was the forerunner of dreaded chimney fires. No self-respecting householder would burn green wood, and that was that.

Insist on having only sound, bright wood of the proper species. Most of the so-called hardwoods are acceptable, while all of the softwoods that I know of make poor fuel. In these times, because of the dread Dutch elm tree disease, elm wood is plentiful, but it is not desirable as fuel. It can be used, but the large body wood is almost impossible to split, and the limb wood produces very little heat.

Apple and pear are perhaps the best, for besides being hard and full of B.T.U's, they give off a delightful fragrance as they burn. White birch is also fragrant, and the oily bark burns with almost explosive violence, but it is not as good as yellow birch for fuel. Just as good—perhaps a bit better—than yellow birch is hard maple, while red or soft maple is slightly inferior. Black cherry and ash are both good for fuel, but both have the disagreeable and dangerous characteristic of popping as they burn, shooting out burning embers. Beech is another prime fireplace wood as are most of the oaks, but I have had little firsthand experience with oak.

None of the members of the willow family, which includes the numerous poplars, produce wood worth burning; eschew it. All of the softwoods in my experience are quick burning and explosive as they burn, popping sparks all over the place, (hemlock is the worst) useful principally as kindling wood. Don't let any poplars or willows or alders or softwoods creep into the cord of wood you are going to pay good money for. The same goes for soggy or dozy or rotten wood. Rotting is but another form of burning, and you will find your wood all burned up before you throw it on the fire if you let them put dozy wood off on you. In general, all the woods with a weight per cubic foot of 45 pounds or over make the best firewood.

Remember that a cord consists of 128 cubic feet. If you are offered a cord of good, sound, bright firewood at a price which seems below the market, be sure that you are not buying a "stove" cord, or a "two-foot" cord. A "stove" cord consists of 16-inch chunks and contains approximately 43 cubic feet, and obviously a "two-foot" cord is but a half a cord. Each of these is worth more than one-third or one-half of the price of a full cord, because of the additional labor involved, but buy them with your eyes open.

Finally, if you want to keep a fire going in your fireplace overnight, the first requisite is plenty of ashes. Deep ashes are the bane of andiron shanks, for they hold the heat around the metal, and sooner than you think these metal bars will be eroded away or broken. But it is just this property of holding heat which will keep the coals alive. We do not use andirons in the fireplace which is in constant use; an air trough scooped in the ashes serves just as well.

Whenever the time of year comes around for an open fire again, I anticipate the joy of lifting a lot of bright, dry wood off the rack to place it on the fire, poke it with the wrought-iron trident I made in my forge, blow the embers with the bellows and then, as the flames curl up, ever gaining in strength, to sit back and relax, and dream perhaps.

The rules for building a fireplace are as follows: The ratio between the area of the fireplace opening and the flue section area should be somewhere between ten and fifteen to one. You can use a commercial throat damper and simplify the construction. The opening of the throat should be as far forward as possible and the nearer the front you can get it, the better. A fireplace should be flared, with the front opening at five feet requiring a fireback of four feet. Since most of the heat from a fireplace is radiant heat, the flare gives a wider angle of emission. For the same reason the fireplace should be no deeper than is necessary to contain the fire, and the fire-back should slope forward. Beyond the damper there should be a smoke shelf at least as wide as the damper, and the sides of the smoke chamber should slope gradually upwards to the first tile and should be smooth.

As for the masonry itself, if stones are abundant they are the cheapest material to use, in spite of the fact that they require more mortar to lay than do bricks. The type of stone used is somewhat dependent on the stone available and also on the taste of the builder. However, the best kind of stone masonry is the kind that would stand, even though there were no mortar to hold it together, and this requires flat stones. For my taste they make a better looking job as well; I am not a devotee of the peanut-brittle type of masonry. If stones are not locally available, bricks are in order. In fact if space is a factor to be considered, their use is more practical than stone. In using bricks, if care is used to see that each course is plumb and level and that the thickness of mortar between bricks is constant, that joints are broken, and that the corners are square and plumb, the chimney will go up—perhaps slowly, but surely, and when completed it can be an achievement to be proud of.

In some areas you may find an old stone or brick house, or one that has bricks between the studs. Many of these conform in general to the uniformity of good taste that seems to have characterized the master builders of the eighteenth and nineteenth centuries, and are still structurally sound. Of course, the restoration of masonry houses presents a much more specialized and precarious problem, and it is likely to prove uneconomic if there are serious faults in the walls or foundations.

After 1850 the "balloon type" of construction became the general rule.

In this type the familiar sawed framing lumber of today came into use, such as "two by fours", "two by eights" and similar dimensions of cutting the boards. The studs or uprights extended from foundation to eaves, and the floor joists for the second story were spiked to them. This method of construction had serious shortcomings, and soon gave way to the "platform" type used in frame houses today.

In the old days, in addition, there were plank houses, with outside walls of vertical planks covered by boards running horitzontally, and others with outside walls of planks placed on their sides, resulting in walls of solid wood six or eight inches thick.

Probably the kind of old house most people are likely to get will be the timber-frame house. Because the weight is carried by the heavy frame, almost any partition may be removed without damaging the strength of. the floors, and almost any repairs can be done economically, if you are not fussy about every floor being level and every wall plumb. All that is required is to have some practical rule-of-thumb workman in charge and your local country craftsmen, one of whom is still likely to be a combination combination carpenter mason.

Intelligent decisions have to be made as to what needs doing and needs not be done. In most instances you can be guided by the judgment of your builder, remembering that if you insist on standards set by the suburban homes of Scarsdale or the apartment dwellings of Park Avenue you will end up dissatisfied with the work done and with a great deal of unneccessary expense.

I am reluctant to leave the subject of country dwellings without a word on the conversion of barns into residences. I have rebuilt many myself, and my son now lives in one he remade several years ago.

The most beautiful of all is the barn I converted in Dummerston, Vermont, for Frances and Robert Flaherty, the filmmaker, creator of *Man of Aran, Nanook of the North* and other lovely and moving films. It was the fourth barn I had redone, and it turned out to be possessed of magical acoustics, and we spent memorable days there with stimulating conversation and glorious music. It was one of the most exciting and rewarding epochs of my life, for not only did the challenge presented bring out the best that was in me, but also warm personal relationships ensued.

People ask about old barns whether the smell of manure persists, and whether rats stay along with the empty grain bins. They do not; for one thing, rats go where the supply of food is.

The most important reason for remodeling barns into dwellings is that in doing so something of beauty is retained. Eric Sloane, the author of the completely charming book, *An Age of Barns,* puts it: "A man farmed to feed his own household and his livestock, and the closeness to the soil and awareness of Nature were an inherent part of American living. This era has nearly gone now—we are at the end of our 'age of barns.'" One cannot be expected to save a barn from destruction merely for the sake of preserving a monument to a way of life now gone, but if this can be done while turning it into a thing of beauty, and a place to live as well, one is powerfully moved to do just that.

Old barns without exception, even in their most decrepit states, are things of beauty, both as simply-proportioned structures and as buildings that were made in a special and rugged way, with beautiful skeletons. These skeletons need not be covered up and lost in reconstruction; in fact, they enhance the design.

Another reason for re-conversion is expense. Nowadays the costs of materials and labor and the difficulty of finding funds to finance the job often impose insupportable obstructions. As things now stand, unless one is fairly wealthy, the only way to get oneself a home in the country is to settle for a pre-fabricated house or even a mobile home. I do not mean to snoot either of these, and surely there are people who would prefer to have a flimsy, undistinguished pre-fab or a shiny new trailer to any crooked, dirty place in which hay had been stored and in which pigs and cows had lived. But the perpendicularity of the lines or the levelness of the floors really make not the slightest difference to those who live in the place.

These are things which are referred to in the most derogatory way by contractors who do not choose to fool with any crazy mess presented by an old barn. Nevertheless, the fact remains that when you start with a barn structure you have the frame and the roof, and quite often the foundation as well. And don't let anyone tell you that these are not valuable assets. He who is intrigued by the idea of remodeling a barn will be told by almost everyone he consults that it would be cheaper to start from scratch. But as far as the cost per cubic foot is concerned, and assuming reasonable and decent workmanship, money can be saved in the renovation and less cash outlay will be required, before the bank will be able to see there is something here which will secure his loan.

It is even possible to move an old barn to a new site, and not impractical for barns are not often hooked up to utilities, and the way they are built adds to the ease of moving them.

In Vermont, most of the good old barns date from the period from 1840 to 1850 when the rural population here was at its height. Most of these, now well over one hundred years old, were built of handhewn timbers for framing, and their sides were covered with boards from local sawmills, many of them ripped from the log with an up-and-down saw. There was a central ramp and barn floor, a bay on either side, and overhead a scaffolding which also served to hold hay and grain as did the bays. Often a hillside location provided for a ground floor which served as quarters for the critters—all except pigs and poultry. These invariably were housed separately. In some of the structures the barn floor was on one side, with bays in the middle and the cow stables on the far side.

But whatever the minor variations in plan, they were framed of timbers hewn by hand, generally eight by eights of native spruce, which were put together in sections or "bents" on the ground, and then raised into place on the foundations. The timbers were fastened together by mortises and tenons, pegged with hardwood pegs, and were profusely braced. This type of construction produced a rigid frame which was infinitely stronger than that of modern "balloon-framed" buildings. These old frames are so strong that they often continue to stand, firm and true, even though the foundations have crumbled out from under them. They will stand just as long as a tight roof keeps the water out. It is this built-in rigidity which makes them easy to move.

So you see the advantages the old barns possess. And knowing these things, perhaps you will be willing to undertake saving one from the fate of abandonment and desertion. There is nothing special about living in them when the job is completed, except there is more room than one might otherwise be able to afford, and the places have a special style and air of their own, which could not be imitated.

The question of size as well as the selection of a location is worth discussing. Certain few rural operations, such as commercial orchards, commercial cattle raising, lumbering operations , and the like require large tracts of land, by their very nature. Even milk production to be profitable requires a herd of at least twenty milkers, and tillage and forage for such a herd or larger requires fairly large tracts of land. On the whole, however, in the case of most of the ways of making a living in the country, including many types of farming, great tracts of land are not required. There are a few well-established precepts to go by: in the first place, intensive cultivation is better than extensive cultivation. The more land owned the more accrues in taxes on the land, but the more seclusion you can have.

People moving to the country used to believe that it wasn't necessary to own vast tracts of land, nor did they want to, with the added burden of taxes. The tendency to acquire more land than could properly be handled resulted in a purchaser's becoming "land poor." The danger was that one's activities on the land be spread so thin that much work was left undone, and the land suffered.

Now, people who are buying country property tend to buy more land than they "need," but for reasons of self-protection. In some areas the back-to-the-country movement is so rapid that frequently large parcels must be obtained to insure the seclusion people are seeking. This is especially true of Vermont and other vacation areas where developments and resort centers are becoming numerous.

Some people have had the misfortune to acquire non-productive land or "sub-marginal" land. Don't buy many acres of such land merely for the sake of being a landowner.

Abandoned farms are bound to be of interest to some prospective purchasers of rural property whose primary interest is not in commercial farming, because they can be purchased cheaply. Common sense must be applied to the consideration of such properties. The abandonment was often the result of an over-all trend developing from changing transportation facilities, improved farm machinery methods, shifting markets, and above all, from changes in our way of living. Just because a farm has been abandoned is not a valid reason for dismissing it as a possibly satisfactory home in the country. If the buildings are adequate and the location satisfactory, many of the ways of making a living in the country which will be discussed later can be satisfactorily conducted on a once abandoned farm.

On the other hand, it is well to remember as far as farming operations are concerned, that if experienced farmers have failed, inexperienced persons have little chance of success unless they have plenty of money and help for reviving the farm.

Whether you plan to farm or not, all of the land owned should be put to some use. It is an offense against agricultural economy to acquire good tillage and take it out of use, but in many instances fields which have been tilled in the past should never have been tilled at all, and such lands can profitably and properly be put to growing trees.

All land should be maintained at its proper and efficient use with proper regard for the requirements of nature.

Living with a new life-style (comments and conclusions)

As a newcomer to country living you will find many differences between country ways and city ways. Many facets of living will turn out to be surprisingly different. You will discover that your quantities of weekly buying will probably go up, for staples especially, and of course the produce from your own place and the other sources of fresh fruit and vegetables in your neighborhood will be stored in greater quantities than you would have been accustomed to in the city.

Distances to travel, poor road conditions in snowy or muddy weather, sudden storms and emergencies, even sudden visitors all mean that you will have to learn to put in larger supplies.

There used to be times at our place in Landgrove when, because of heavy snows, we have not been able to get out for two weeks at a time. There should be no emergency that will seriously disturb the country housewife. She should be able upon any occasion to whip up a hearty and palatable meal, for the parson, the county agent, the veterinarian, or the stranded neighbor.

There will be a tendency to spend less money, and prices and values will be scrutinized more carefully. This will lead you to the catalogs of mail-order houses. No country family is completely equipped without the catalogs, and they are apt to be in fairly constant use. You will find that shopping by mail is a satisfactory way of doing business; and you will be glad that you can send for everything from a compost shredder to seeds, from clothes to pencils, and all is delivered almost to your door.

In fact all the casual expenses of daily living will be less in the country than in the city. In the city a ten-dollar bill, once broken, has a miserable habit of mysteriously disappearing, leaving nothing tangible behind to show that it ever was there. Bus fare, movies, petty self-indulgences, lunches, tips, shoe shines, goodness knows what all. Of this there is none in the country. It is not even necessary to carry money in your pocket; nay, it is not even wise to do so, for it is too easy to lose it. It can fall out if you climb over walls in the woods or through fences when you go through the fields, or if you go down under a car to help a neighbor

83

who is stuck. It can drop out of your pocket without your ever noticing it if you happen to run and leap and turn handsprings with the children because you are all so glad to be living in the country now.

There will be other changes in your habits of daily life. The chances are that the family will be home together more than in the past, that the men folk will eat three meals a day with the rest of the family, that everyone will get up earlier and go to bed earlier, and even that the head of the family will do as I do and snatch forty winks of sleep during his "nooning."

Almost every country place purchased will have trees growing somewhere. If not a woods with merchantable timber in it, at least a wood lot. Many of the old, abandoned farms will have wild land growing up to trees and old pastures with the forest creeping in at the edges. If you have trees at all you are fortunate, for while they impose a responsibility on you, they are also a very important source of income potential if not actual. Sometimes the trees will not be ready as a salable crop for twenty or thirty years, especially if they are part of one of the reforestation projects which was sponsored by the then Soil Conservation service back in the 'forties and 'fifties. Do not regard your trees from a sentimental point of view as many city dwellers do, and swear that as long as you own them never a tree shall be cut. Trees are like all other living organisms, they are young, they mature, and they sicken and die. Mature trees are better cut and used than left standing, only to eventually disintegrate. Some of the stands of trees on your place are ripe for improvement cutting; while not mature, the undesirable species, the malformed or diseased trees, may be cut and used for fuel. Such a cutting gives the owner an immediate return and improves the chances of the remaining trees to mature. If you have timber suitable for use, see if the stand cannot be placed on a sustained yield basis. If you have old pastures and mowings which will never be pastured or tilled, consider the possibility of setting them out to trees, and starting a "Tree Farm."

Whatever your situation is as far as the trees on your place are

concerned, do not forget that they are a part of your responsibility to the land and to nature. Farm forestry is a very important part of owning farm lands, and it is a subject that no land owner can afford to ignore. In any state the State Forest Service will be glad to be of service to you. Many states maintain regional or county foresters who will be at your service. Where there are Natural Resources Soil Conservation Districts, farm forestry is part of the general program. In many cases seedlings may be had either very cheaply or free, for the setting up of plantations on your wild lands. In some states the establishment of such plantations will make the land tax exempt. If you have timber to cut, the forest service will surely inspect your stand free of charge, and give you a cutting plan. Be wise about your woods, and do something about them and talk over all the possibilities with a professional forester before you make your decisions.

There is no doubt but that more and more people are turning to the country hoping and believing that in that direction lies a normal and satisfying life. Over the years many people have come to our house to get help and advice about living in the country. Many of them have sworn that they will not go back to their old routines in the cities. Many of them are mature men with families. Many are professional men. Perhaps this trend is an indication that our philosophy of civilization is changing, and our material values are giving place to spiritual ones. If this is so, it is a good sign indeed, but for the moment, at least, we find ourselves caught on the horns of a dilemma; we want our machines but we do not want to live the kind of a life that our machines force us to lead. Unless we go way into debt, we cannot afford all the cars and tractors and electrical gadgets we think we need; the enslavement to machines they impose upon us is debilitating; the pollution they cause is intolerable.

Many of those who leave the city and come to the country to live have a sufficient income to live on. They may have started their trips away from the city as skiers or vacationers, and then later decided to buy property in a place that they liked to visit. They have few of the problems of the people who come to the country to make a living and in many instances their dollar will stretch much further in the country than it will in the city, and they are in a very strong position. This book is not addressed to such people.

This book is addressed to those who want to live in the country and who will have to make their living there. To them I say again that to live a well-adjusted and successful life in the country it is very probable that many of the old standards of value will have to be changed. There will have to be a shift in point of view and a deliberate decision to assume a new style of life.

I have failed if I have not made this point clear. I want to extol the advantages and benefits of country living, for I believe in them. I want to help every one that I possibly can to a way of living as satisfactory and complete as the one that I have found. My position is realistic and fraught with common sense only if the facts are viewed from the same point of view as I view them. If you want to live in the country be sure that you are being tough-minded about it. Be of good courage but do not ever say that I did not tell you what you were getting in for.

Part two

Preface

Since this book was first written there has been an incredible transformation in the ways of farming, and in this part of the country such an upsurge in land prices—along with formidable increases in taxes—that cheap land is not to be had, and only those farms operating under the most favorable conditions can remain in business. In fact, it is quite probable that in Vermont, at least, the days of the farms are numbered.

Nevertheless those who have the means to acquire the land can come to the country and till the soil, but what their efforts add up to will not be farming in the present meaning of the term, where the words "farm factory" might more properly describe farming operations. So, while I do not dismiss "farming" as a possible means of sustaining life, I must in all honesty state that the amount of capital needed to set one's self up in such an enterprise is at least ten times as much now as it was when I first wrote the chapter in Part II on farming.

Furthermore, in localities where the recreation influx has taken place, lands once appraised on the basis of their ability to produce, which was the measure of how much a purchaser was willing to pay per acre, are now appraised on the basis of recent sales in the neighborhood. The prices paid for these recreational acres reflect the ability of the purchaser to obtain what he wants, and such prices as these people are willing to pay simply make it impossible for the farmer to compete for additional land or even to pay the new taxes based on "fair market value."

With the change-over to a recreational economy in Vermont or in any rural area, all the occupations having to do with services to the public multiply in both number and kind. Of particular importance are those areas in mountainous states which are suitable for winter sports where a larger and ever larger portion of the local economy is supported by the ski business. In waterside areas the proportion supported by boating and water sports is also increasing. The interest in skiing and other winter sports has of course increased enormously in the past twenty-five years, and the end of the growth does not yet seem to be in sight.

Another aspect of the recreational economy is the need for labor, both skilled and unskilled, and in these days and times, even the unskilled are reasonably well paid but the employment is apt to be seasonal, and thus might not produce a year-around competence, however modest it might be. Nevertheless the laborer who has a job on the ski-slopes in the winter-time may very well find himself a job with a building contractor in the summer and fall, and if his scale of values has been adjusted to frugality and simplicity, he may thus be able to get along.

In the chapter on "Selling and Handicrafts" I speak of The Vermont Country Store which now has become famous nation-wide, a place where honest and hard-to-find merchandise is sold at reasonable prices. As a mail-order store it is surely the largest in Vermont, and its catalogue, "The Voice of the Mountains," is a collector's item. Stores patterned after this one have sprung up all over the country, often as natural food stores, organic produce markets or ecology action centers. With good planning, frugality and simplicity a man can get along with a business like this, too.

Actually what has been taking place here in the rural east for several decades seems to have set a pattern which is being repeated in many other places in the country where resorts have been started. A recent article datelined Lovel, Wyoming, entitled "Now a Land Rush in the West as City Folks Stake Claims," describes a new epidemic of land fever which has now hit the American West. What first happened in the East is now happening in the rush for land in the West, and the same old problems are again arising. The people who are established regard with apprehension the influx of new settlers, for with their advent all the things these people cherished are diminished, if not destroyed altogether. A dilemma is born of the widespread yearning for some land and for escape and at the same time a longing to preserve the wild country. So the real estate agents sharpen up their ball-points and with their eyes on the quick buck they sign up the hordes who want to move in.

The sad part of it is that if left undirected, this urge for the wild areas is quite likely to spawn the same evils that the escapees are fleeing. The polluted streams and garish commercial establishments follow along like the camp followers of old. I'm afraid that the whole business is a logical development arising out of industrialization and mechanization: had the old patterns been allowed to stand the need to escape from the shambles would not exist, and man's relationships with nature would have remained natural and in many cases beautiful as well. But what is, is; and perhaps these things can be worked out before too much desecration is committed.

The United States of America is a big place and no doubt there are areas where the mechanization of farming on good farm land has led to the availability of some other sub-marginal farm lands that bring lower land prices. These lands, and lands going for taxes, are being bought now by young people beginning to homestead. They are also looking into the possibilities of the public lands that are for sale.

When I first wrote This Country Life twenty-five years ago, we did not have electricity in the house. When I mentioned the freeze locker, I referred to the locker one could rent in a nearby town. Without electricity this home was a different sort of place from what it is now with all its myriads of electrical devices. While it would be impossible to return to the days not so far back in the past, let no one believe that life has been changed *in any essential way for the better. In fact the contrary might prove to be the case, for in becoming dependent upon our machines we have lost something which perhaps outweighs our relief from labor, and that is knowledge that labor is sweet. Moreover, in acceding to the blandishments of technology, we have let ourselves get out of step with nature.*

Part II ends with the query "Where are We Heading?"—the question which is the most important one confronting the human race today. Times are critical, and men of probity and wisdom are in the tiny minority. Their being outvoted is and must be taken for granted. The belief that truth resides in simple numbers, and that there is no evil in the world are both dangerous and stupid. The principle that the founding fathers established was that sovereignty rested with the people and their attempt to implement the means for the exercise of this power contained no ingredients of "true democracy."

All very complicated perhaps, but the words in the Vermont Constitution which stipulate that he who is elected to represent the people in the Legislature be he "who is most noted for his wisdom and his virtue" points up my meaning. True, small town meetings represent the nearest thing we have to true democracy, but even here there were originally conditions imposed on the granting of the franchise, and with the eroding of these and with the concentrations of populations there is very little true democracy left, even here.

—o—

As long as we deliberately follow false principles, the quality of our government is certain to worsen and the establishment of a true democracy, which will only serve to place the power in the hands of the demagogues, will result eventually in pure dictatorship.

And even here one could be convinced that the government might be less venal if the power fell into the hands of a wise and noble man. But that this should ever occur is improbable, for those who seek power are either truly evil in their lust or else bemused by a rank mysticism which self-selects them as the Messiah. As a matter of fact, common sense must agree that he who seeks elected office in this country, is by that very fact disqualified from holding office. Crazy? Think it over.

Farming

THE FIRST JOB most people think of for country living is farming, and sometimes they do and sometimes they do not consider that the hardest of all jobs in the country is that of farming. The farmer must be an agronomist and husbandman first, and a business man and executive second. In addition he must be a good mechanic, with skills in carpentry, plumbing, masonry, wiring, automotive repairs, rigging, roofing, and painting. The professional skills of the economist, the civil engineer, the accountant, the veterinarian, and the meterologist are inescapably his province as well.

But that is not the worst of it by any means; he must also have an adequate supply of capital wherewith to finance his operations and good relations with the banks that will lend him the advances he needs.

In fact the requirements of experience and capital are so severe and demanding, that I do not believe it possible for a person from the city with neither experience nor adequate capital to come to the country and make a go of farming as his only occupation. When young people today move as a group to a place in the country, it is usual for one or more of them to have another job or else some capital or an allowance to live on.

In the business world the current tendency is toward specialization, and in the business of farming this specialization has grown to be twofold: first in the direction of a single money crop, and secondly in the direction of specialized operations on the part of the farmer himself. The result is a commercialized agriculture, and the setting up of "farm factories." The acceptance of the farm-factory concept is now widespread in this country, and it is the basis of most of our current thinking on farm subjects, dismal and wrongheaded as much of it is.

If you accept the farm-factory idea, then it is reasonable to expect that a proper factory, efficiently run, turning out a merchandizable commodity, will produce a profit. Energy, business brains, and adequate capital should be the requirements for success in such an enterprise. This seems to be a fairly widespread conviction, but it is one which I do not believe can be justified as a proper concept for running a farm, at least not in this part of the country where I am familiar with farming conditions.

This doctrine of farming as an industry, of farm factories, is preached by the United States Department of Agriculture, and it has been disseminated through the land-grant colleges, the Extension Services, the Farm Bureaus, and the County Agents for half a century or more. All the great organized farm groups have accepted it for the most part; farm lobbies in our National and State legislatures strive for farm-factory objectives; many farmers themselves accept it. Few and far between are the voices raised in opposition to the concept of farming as a business which uses the living earth and the fragile life chains as the raw material to be manufactured into the farm product.

The existence of farm subsidies, and the many very real agricultural problems which confront us, should give us pause to think. It seems to me that the basic fallacy in our current thinking on farm matters is the assumption made that nature is a constant, not a variable in the agricultural equation to put it in the mathematical terms of the economist.

There are three extremely variable components of nature, as applied to farming. These are man, weather, and soil. The reply may be made that the farmer can and will be educated to the point where he becomes an efficient business man, that crop insurance will iron out the variations in weather, and that greater perfection in the manufacture and application of fertilizers will nail the land down to a non-variable.

These answers are in line with our American tradition of technological progress, with the widely accepted belief that mechanical devices or herbicidal or other attacks by man will turn the trick. Why will not business machines and accounting systems do for the farmer, why will not actuarial computations properly applied compensate for crop failure, and why will not scientific knowledge chemically substitute for the microscopic and multitudinous activity of the soil? We believe in progress, do we not? Well then, technological advance will lead us to the solution of our problems, people piously proclaim.

We in America have accepted the eighteenth century doctrine of progress as has no other country in the world. Let me quote from "Farmers in a Changing World": "It [the idea of progress] had begun, indeed, as an intellectual doctrine but soon became an unreasoned basic attitude, an assumption that the very law of nature itself compelled man and society to go on improving indefinitely.... The doctrine of technological progress, from being merely the idea of a few intellectuals, rapidly became a widely accepted popular assumption."

Though many people still do not question this doctrine of technological progress, the time has arrived when many others are doing a great deal of tough-minded thinking on the subject. To them it is apparent that something is basically wrong. The fact that so many people are dissatisfied with modern conditions of living; that so many are turning toward the country in their search for normal living is proof of our unease and dissatisfaction. Our mechanical age, which has just turned into the atomic and moon-shot age, has justified all the wildest dreams of mechanical progress, but when it comes to human affairs the accomplishments of the age are very far from impressive.

In any event, on the basis of my personal observation I question the basic doctrine of the farm factory, and I stipulate as requirements for successful farming much more than is demanded by business or industry, and a view of the farm as a living organism like a very complex creature in need of our care and nurture.

The ideal background for a farmer is to have been born on the farm, and his father and grandfather on the same farm before him. Love of the land goes with long tenure, and love of the land goes hand in hand with successful farming. A basic understanding of the processes of nature is born of long and traditional association with nature, and an understanding of nature is necessary for successful farming. Actually the success or failure of a farming operation cannot be determined on the basis of one year, or even several years. Rich virgin soil can be mined, lusty and profitable crops can be taken from the soil year after year, but eventually, if nothing is returned not only will a profitable crop be impossible, but the land poor and sour will not support enough natural growth to prevent erosion, so that the very soil itself is lost. On the other hand soils which have been depleted by greed or ignorance, may, if they are not too far gone, be brought back to profitable tillage. So it is that a good farmer may spend years and money working his land up to the point where it may produce to its maximum capability, while on the other hand a poor farmer, working his farm factory for all it is worth, with the aid of farm subsidies and commercial fertilizers, may extract a decent profit, year after year, depleting the humus and the bacteriological resources of the soil all the while. In fact I will go so far as to state that the profit motive as applied to farming is responsible for our depleted soils, and further, that it is the very essence of the farm-factory point of view.

Hand in hand with the farm-factory notion is the belief that the more acres under cultivation, the bigger the operation, the bigger the profit. The use of modern farm machinery fits hand and glove with this notion. Here again I must disagree. In the first place machines are expensive to maintain, they require more land per unit of growing plant to operate them, and, finally, they do not do the job as well as it can be done by hand. Most important of all, when farm prices are unfavorable, the big farm is in for a bigger licking than the small farm. In fact a small intensively cultivated farm can stay in the black when a large farm with its heavy load of fixed charges must go into the red.

I fully realize that statistics are available to show that a large farm business pays better than a small one. I am aware of the fact that the advice given in official documents on agriculture is that the purchaser should be sure that the farm in question is large enough to produce an income which will provide a satisfactory standard of living.

The answer is, that I question the statistics. Figures can be manipulated so as to prove almost anything, and in the case in question the variables are so imponderable and there are so many of them, that I seriously question the value of the figures offered.

When this book was first written, it was possible for me to write estimates for a farm operation with a basic figure of $15,000 and this included $5,000 for land and buildings, $5,000 for stock and equipment with the other $5,000 the cash reserve for backlog and emergencies. Now, anyone aiming for a self-sufficient dairy farm, for example, would expect he had to have a herd of fifty cows, the 200 acres to support them, and the $25,000 worth of equipment to go with it. If his land costs him $500 an acre—which it may do in areas of rich crop land—, there is $100,000 for the farm; if the Holsteins he decides on cost $500 also, a herd of fifty will come to $25,000. In addition he may plan for a $15,000 tractor, a truck as well as a family car, and, if he has woodlands, a power saw, perhaps.

Though it is obvious that these modern high figures reflect the attitude of a farm factory operation, it is nevertheless true with today's price structures that the alternative is a modest homestead farm, on the subsistence level, with no aim to make a living, but with every possibility of making a way of life. I will confess that my approach has been a pessimistic one, and that my attitudes and opinions are at odds with current ideas about farming as a business. But I am aware that more and more young people are turning to homesteading and living off the land as their way of life. Whatever brings a man to it, I still believe that for the right persons farming offers the most satisfactory way of making a living.

He who would make a living at farming must first of all love his soil and his animals. His devotion in this direction should outweigh his preoccupation with making a profit. His interest in the land and all that grows thereon, including crops and animals, is not enough however. Along with his interest must go a manual dexterity, and a facility for handling animals. To maintain a farm plant and all the equipment that goes with it requires constant tinkering, and if the farmer does not like animals and, what is more important, if animals do not like him, he will not do well with them. This would be a serious upsetting of the family and group life on the farm, a detriment to the productive capacities of the farm, and, for the fields and gardens, a loss of the manure which the animals produce, and the compost that is made from it.

In addition no one need seriously consider making a life for himself or a living at farming if he dislikes hard work and long hours. Since much of a farmer's work is laborious and monotonous, both endurance and patience are required if the work is to be done well. In fact, I believe that it is necessary that a man actually enjoy the work, and look forward daily to being outdoors with his animals, poultry and gardens, and to the pride and pleasure he will feel in his fine crops and healthy stock.

One year his heifers will delight him; another it will be his lettuce, especially if it is one I grew a few years ago, *Le Merveille des Quatres Saisons,* which shows sturdy growth and even development. Its colors of red, purplish-red, pink and varying shades of green will enhance the splendor of the heads, which will stand evenly matched at 14 inches high and make a solid row. In comparison to other colored lettuces like *Ruby,* this marvel of France will surprise the grower by being of the uttermost tenderness and of the most delicious flavor. Since I sell my lettuce to two near-by restaurants from the first week in June for as long as it lasts, the 300 feet of rows I had that year delighted the customers at them both for several weeks. By mid-July the garden is yielding edible pod peas (after their lovely lavender blossoms,) tiny tender carrots and beets and the crops of spinach, broccoli and cabbages that come along later. All this bounty of a garden greatly offsets the hard work and patience required to keep it in top form.

At my garden there have always been many visitors, and I am happy that in showing people around I have not had to be apologetic about anything. The garden is in fact a lovely thing to see, and the first words spoken by the viewers have inevitably been "It's beautiful," and in speaking of gardens, there are no more encouraging words to the gardener than these.

If you take such delights in farm work, and are not fazed by all that farming and gardening will demand of you personally and physically, and

if your inclinations and talents lie in these directions, then you are ready
to embark on the many practical routes to getting started.

Of the two factors, experience and capital, in my opinion capital is
the more important. You will need money not merely to enable you to
buy the proper farm along with its appurtenances, but you will need some
cash behind you during the first few uncertain years of the venture.

The amount of money that you will need will depend upon the type
and size of operation which you plan to take on. In the first place there
is a tendency to pay more for farms than they are actually worth. In many
places people now regard farm land, and especially forest land, as recreational and vacation land also, and this has boosted prices still higher. At
the present time this must be particularly guarded against for farm prices
keep on going up and up, and speculative forces govern more and more
of the factors determining costs and farm taxes go up and up, too—often
to the extent that a farmer simply cannot afford to stay in business any
longer.

Even so, careful search for hill farms or farms out of production for
a decade or so will often result in the discovery of a good buy. If some
of the family have capital or have other jobs, a fine and joyous way of
life can be established at one of these old places. When credit is available,
it is certainly welcome, but to overburden a new and perhaps doubtful
venture with heavy interest charges is unwise unless some of the family
do have other jobs. I believe that the tendency to borrow to the hilt should
be guarded against as being of more potential danger to the borrower than
to the lender. It is usually wiser to curb one's desires for more and revise
one's needs so that less will do instead.

When it comes to the final questions of land value, the true value
is sometimes difficult to determine. There is one source of information,
nevertheless, that should not be neglected: the current appraised valuation
of the property. When you have checked this valuation, then determine,
if possible, what per centum of real value this figure represents in the
eyes of the appraisers. Sometimes it is a matter of law; sometimes of

custom. Look also into the record of the land itself, and look up the old deeds to see what record there is of the actual figure at which past transactions took place. The mortgage record of the land also gives valuable information.

What you may actually expect to pay in terms of dollars per acre, it is impossible to predict. Prices and values vary widely in all parts of the country. The elements which enter into computing the actual land value are several. First of all there is the soil proper, whether rich in plant foods, or lacking; whether stony or stone free; whether flat, and subject to flooding, or steep and subject to erosion; whether well drained or poorly drained; whether based on light sands or heavy clays. Study the soil, get all the dope on it that you can. Next must be considered the climate, the length of the growing season, the amount of rainfall, the possibility of drought. Topography is also a factor which enters into the fixing of value of farm lands, as is nearness to market, transportation facilities, water supply, telephone and electric service. All of these factors have a bearing on the value of farm land. Unfortunately the speculative factor will often enter in as well, so give all factors careful study.

If, after mature deliberation, it is apparent to you that the price asked for the farm you have your eye on is more than it is actually worth, you had best keep looking elsewhere unless you have the good fortune to be able to rent it for a while to try it out. In order to get started right, the prospective farmer must buy, or rent, at prices that are right.

The primary demand upon your stock of capital is the purchase of the farm; the next demand will be for the purchase of equipment and supplies. If the farm purchased is a going concern, the equipment can often be bought along with the farm, even, often times, including the livestock. In any event the amount of capital needed for these purchases will vary depending upon the individual circumstances. A rule of thumb to go by is that the investment in livestock, machinery, feed and supplies, will just about equal the value of the real estate. In other words, if you have a fifty-five thousand dollar farm, you can expect to have another fifty-five thousand dollars invested in equipment, stock and machinery—even as, forty years ago, if you had a five-thousand-dollar farm, you had another five thousand invested in your cows, tractor, tedder and plows. (Such figures, of course, are not for homesteading, but for a dairy farm that will support itself and a good-sized family.)

In addition to these two primary demands on your capital, I would say that there is still a third, and that is a cash reserve. The amount of capital required for this is difficult to arrive at, and it will depend of course on the size of the operation and the demands to be made on it. My guess would be that it should be a sum large enough to permit the farm to keep going for at least five years (again assuming not much outside income besides that to be derived from the farm.) If this reserve is not in cash, but borrowed against the original investment in land and equipment, it should never go above the figure of half of the total value. An investment of a hundred and ten thousand dollars (or of ten thousand) should not become security for loans of more than fifty-five (or of five,) as the case may be.

So much for some suggestions for the capital requirements of getting started in farming. The next thing is to get started in the right way. There are many different farming areas in this great country of ours, and many different kinds of farming to choose from. Within the various areas, as shown in the map below, there are many different kinds and conditions of individual farms to be found.

The ten major areas here shown include various kinds of farming, such as produce farming, milk production, fruit farming, nut tree crops, market gardening and cash crop farming, as well as others.

There will be no attempt here to write a treatise on any one of the many different types of farming, full treatment of which would run into several volumes. Nor is there any idea of turning the city slicker into a farmer in a few easy lessons. Rather, it is a sketchy but sincere attempt to indicate what you are getting yourself in for, if you want to go to farming, and to tell you where you can find helpful material on the subject.

After you get your place, there are incidental expenses you will have to expect. For example, you may need tiles or ditches for drainage or irrigation.

One advantage about raising ducks and geese, if you have a pond, is that if they stay healthy, they require less care and attention than the same number of chickens would. For example, young geese can be put out on a pasture range when they are only a few weeks old, and they will need little additional food as long as the grass is green. If you have a berry patch, put the geese in there. They will eat the weeds, and leave the brambles and canes alone. Be sure to consult your county agent about what breed of goose will be most suitable for your purposes, and the same for ducks if you decide to have them. The county agent will also help you with advice about feeding, housing, wintering and all such matters.

Many small country families have solved the problem of milk by keeping one or two goats. Goat's milk can often be tolerated, it has been discovered, by infants and others who are allergic to other milk. If you get a good dairy goat, she will produce at least two quarts of milk a day for about eight to ten months out of the year. The feed she needs will cost only about one-sixth of the cost of the feed for a dairy cow. And your cost for the goat will be $30 to $80 depending on her breed and her production record, if she has one already. The feed you should give her when she is producing would include all the clover, alfalfa and mixed hay that she will eat, and any available root crops you can spare such as turnips, carrots, beets or parsnips, though good-quality silage, if you have it, can be substituted for the root vegetables. If she can be in pasture, these quantities are not necessary, but in the winter she should get two pounds of good alfalfa or clover hay, a pound and a half of root crops or silage, and one or two pounds of concentrates such as oats, bran, linseed or other protein supplement. Remember that if your goat eats turnips just before milking time, the flavor of your milk is likely to be rather turnipish.

Sheep raising appeals to some country people because it does not involve expensive equipment or heavy labor. You do need plenty of pasture and very good fences, requirements that the small farmer may not be able to meet. In season you will have to separate lambs from ewes, so you need room for pastures for each, as well as space to allow for frequent rotations to clean ground in spring, summer and fall times of year. The fence you will need should be strong enough and high enough to be dog-proof. Often used is woven and barbed wire, 56 to 58 inches high, tightly stretched and close to the ground. Sheep will need a lot of attention, especially at lambing time. Their needs and habits are quite different from other farm animals.

Most beginners start with dual-purpose sheep, using breeds that combine good wool and lamb-producing quality. Again I advise that you consult your county agent, and aim for a good, rather than outstanding, breed unless you intend to sell rams for breeding. Plan to have the lambs born in winter months so that parasites will be discouraged by the cold weather. Plan to buy new ewes in the late summer or early fall, and put them immediately on pasture for late forage.

If you plan to keep a family cow, she will need a sunny, comfortable shelter or stable. If given a box stall of about ten feet square, she may be left untied; though she may also be confined to a smaller place at times, if held with a stanchion, rope or strap. The bedding in a stall should be about three times as much as you use in the smaller space of a stanchion stall. This kind of stall should be provided with a manger and a gutter for droppings with at least 4 or 5 feet behind the gutter to facilitate removal of manure and to make it easy for the cow to get in and out. Always see to it that your cow does not have to stand in a cold draft in the winter and if the sun is out, and the box stall faces south, it is all right to open it to the daylight, except in very cold weather. An enclosed stall should have ventilation from a tilting window on the side opposite to the prevailing wind.

The winter feed for a cow can consist of hay and a mixture of concentrates such as alfalfa, soybean, alside clover or early-cut grass hay. A Jersey or Guernsey will need at least ten pounds of hay a day, and a pound of grain for each two to four pounds of milk she produces. Good to feed with the hay is a mixture of ground corn and wheat bran, plus some soybean oil meal or linseed oil meal for extra protein. Provide your cow with a block of trace mineral salt or add loose salt to her concentrate mix, and give her fresh water twice a day.

In summer she will need more water than that. And she should have two acres of pasture to feed in. Blue grass or mixtures of grass will need supplements when they drop in production. Every three years or five years —in the northern states—pastures can be seeded with alfalfa and ladino clover mixed with grasses. Also for summer pasture in the north, use sudangrass and crosses of sudangrass and sorghum or soybeans. A temporary pasture so made can be planted next to the permanent pasture of blue grass. Do not ever let your cow eat young sudan during its early growth, or during its regrowth just after a frost or a drought. The reason for this is that the sudangrass during this stage of growth might cause prussic acid poisoning.

If you always handle your cow gently and quietly, and see that all her fences are well-constructed, she will stay quiet and not try to break through. One effective fence is made of four barbed wires tightly stretched to good stout posts. Be sure to brush her daily and do not let manure cake on her flanks. This care is especially important whenever she is kept in a stall.

When milking, plan to do it twice a day, keep everything perfectly clean, wiping the udder and flanks with a clean, damp cloth before you milk. Keep your fingernails short and do not insert milk tubes or straws into the teats.

A Jersey or Guernsey cow is usually preferred for a family cow because she is smaller and needs less feed and doesn't give as much milk as the larger breeds like Holsteins, or Brown Swiss. Do not buy a cow that kicks, or that wears a yoke, muzzle or nosepiece. She will have bad habits. Also be sure that the cow you buy is free from tuberculosis, brucellosis and leptispirosis, all of which diseases can be transmitted to man.

If you plan to keep chickens, get day-old chicks in the spring, and raise them in a brooder house. Only order from a reputable hatchery, and have the house warm, the starting mash and water ready and a warm hood for them to get under at night. For the first two days you can feed them cracked baby chick corn and grits; but after that it is usual to switch to mash for the next 4 or 5 weeks, with a little grit mixed in. Allow one inch of space at the feeders and one-half inch at the drinking fountains for each bird, and keep food and water ready for them at all times. Increase the amounts as they grow. Switch to an all-mash growing diet when the chicks are six to eight weeks old, and then add small amounts of grain, increasing that until about 15 weeks they get half mash and half grain. Do not increase the grain percentage too fast, for it hasn't the proteins and vitamins the mash has, and these are especially needed by the chicks when they are young. If you want to mix your own grain from corn, wheat, oats and barley, get directions from your county agent or State extension officer. After they are six weeks old, chicks may be put outdoors to run on a range if the weather is favorable. White Leghorns will start to lay about 20 to 24 weeks; but all-purpose birds suitable for both laying and cooking, such as Rhode Island Reds, begin at about 22 to 26 weeks. About two weeks before you expect them to lay, switch the mash to an all-mash laying diet. Feed layers this mash, plus some grain and grit as well as the oystershells necessary for the calcium supply for making normal eggshells. If normal, a hen will lay 200 to 240 eggs per year. She eats 85 to 115 pounds of feed a year, depending on her breed and weight.

Housing for chickens should be draft-free and well-ventilated, especially in hot weather. Allow 3 to 4 square feet of floor space per bird, and see to it that the roosts are 2 to 3 feet above the floor and 10 to 12 inches apart. Put a pit under the roost, covered with wire netting, to keep the birds away from them. Cover the floor with 6 to 8 inches of absorbent litter for chickens to scratch in, and renew it whenever it gets damp. Always clean and disinfect the house before you get new birds, and always give them fresh litter. Laying hens should be given a box nest for every four or five birds.

If you have woodlands on your farm, it is advisable to get help from a state or county professional forester and to read the publications of the forestry division of the U.S. Department of Agriculture. You may need advice about thinning, pruning, girdling or preparing the soil for improving your stand of trees, letting in the sunlight and improving the moisture-retaining capacities of your forest floor so that seed germination possibilities are at their best.

You may want to consult about reseeding, starting new woodland areas, growing evergreens or building water bars to prevent erosion on old logging roads. New evergreen plantings have been put in by many landowners for multiple benefits such as control of brush, erosion control, and eventually the tree crop—whether for Christmas trees or wood products. The USDA Farmers Bulletin 2187 and the Agricultural Information Bulletin 278 both give many hints about forest care and forest production.

There are other products besides wood from the forest. Find out what is edible in the woods you have. Maybe there are nuts of various kinds: walnuts, beechnuts, hickory nuts, butternuts, pinyon nuts. And maybe your land and climate are suitable for planting nut groves. Chestnuts, if you can grow a blight-free variety, are a good cash crop. If you decide to plant a walnut grove, keep a flock of sheep, too, to mow the grass and to give you fleece and meat also. You are very likely to have wild grapes in the woods and along the hedgerows in some areas, or pawpaws or persimmons in others, or cranberries or plums in other terrains and locations. Perhaps you even have ginger or ginseng growing on your land.

In certain areas you can harvest florists' materials from the forest floor. In the southern mountains the farmers gather galax, leucothoe, mountain laurel, cones and evergreens. In the Pacific northwest they harvest salal and huckleberry. In season, many local residents make wreaths and sprays where the materials are abundant, and sell holly as well as balsam branches and cone wreaths. Vermonters pick ferns to send to market, and it makes a fascinating occupation, taking one far into the cool depths of the forests, a lonesome and lovely business.

Sometimes florists are not averse to receiving plant materials from species that are on the conservation list of protected plants in various states. Consult the list in your state before you pick (or dig up) forest plants, and be wary of the items suggested in the USDA Bulletin   278; it contains protected plants.

If you don't mind people coming to your place, there are many other uses of your land for profit taken up in later chapters.

In conclusion I quote from circular 108, "Selecting a Farm in Vermont," to which I have already referred.

"Experience on a successful farm is the best way to learn the business of farming. As a general rule, sons of successful farmers who continue to farm, follow their fathers' example, and become successful farmers. Contrary to common opinion, farming is not a simple vocation. A farmer must be able to combine all the factors of production into a successful and smoothly running farming unit. This involves having the ability to handle farm workers and show them how to do the various farm jobs. It involves not only having knowledge of principles and practices of business management, of plant growth, of feeding and care of livestock, of maintenance of soil fertility and of handling machinery, but also the ability to translate that knowledge into effective operation.

"Many individuals who have been successful in other business undertakings feel that because of their success in these undertakings they could be successful farmers. This is not necessarily true, since farming is very different from any other business. There are few industries which require such a wide range of knowledge and ability as farming."

Selling and handicrafts

For those who have had experience at selling there are many opportunities in the country to put this experience to gainful use, whether they find ways to sell country things to the city or to city visitors passing through, or whether they bring city things to sell in the country. The ex-urbanite will find at times that he is in an advantageous position, because of his connections in the city, to sell country products there. He may act as agent or middleman for others, or he may be a producer, selling his own specialties directly to the city or to the city visitor.

The opportunities for acting as agent selling country products to the city will vary in the various parts of the country. Each individual will have to look around him and size up the possibilities. It would be an impossible task for me to cover the nationwide aspects of country selling, but I am able to give some concrete suggestions.

There is in several northern states and in Canada an opportunity to do something with maple products, even during bad seasons because of bad weather there are almost no maple products available. In normal times the right person living in a district where sugaring is done can do his neighbors a service and make a profit for himself. In the first place, pure maple syrup is so far superior to its various imitations and substitutes that it can be regarded as an extra fine food specialty. If properly packaged, graded, and distributed to outlets specializing in quality goods, an excellent business can be built up, I am certain. Sometimes the small producer puts his syrup up in gallon cans, which are not suitable for the quality trade for two reasons; first of all the size of the package is too large, and secondly, it is unattractive. If syrup were put up in specially designed glass containers from half pints to quarts, it would be more salable and would command a fancy price.

Though there are state laws and federal standards to be met, some producers are not exacting enough as to the color and weight of their product, and there will be a wide variation in the quality of their syrup. More rigid supervision during the making of the syrup, and grading of the finished product, would enable the purchaser to buy, knowing exactly what he was getting. A person with some experience in selling, and with

111

connections in the city could find a market for all the fancy packaged syrup that his immediate neighborhood would produce. Other maple products such as hard sugar, soft sugar, and maple candies are also products for this type of selling.

The forest products mentioned in the last chapter can become a good base for someone who is properly located and has connections in the city. Ferns and other non-evergreen plant materials and sprays are needed by florists. Of the same general character and imposing roughly the same requirements of locations is the business of collecting and selling of evergreens, which are the stock in trade of the occupation. Christmas trees might be included, but there are certain peculiarities attendant upon Christmas tree business which disqualify it to my notion, unless you have an excellent local or nearby market. Briefly, the season is short, the article bulky, and the outlets are more or less unstable. Dealing in other greens, even for the Christmas trade, does not have the same disadvantages.

Certain low evergreens, balsam, spruce, and pine boughs and cones —either plain or made up into wreaths and sprays—are in demand over a longer season, and their sale is through florists' shops.

In many places where balsam fir abounds some of the natives put in spare moments at making balsam pillows. I believe the market for this sort of thing could be developed. Particularly if more care and taste were used in making the finished product. In all such operations the principal function of the agent, besides selling, is to grade and standardize the product as well as to see that it is attractively put up.

A field which seems to me to be particularly undeveloped is that of collecting and selling plants and herbs which are found in the woods and fields. In this instance the job would be for someone who knew or who could find out the requirements of the trade as to certain essential oils, and then survey the countryside with an eye to developing its possibilities. As an instance, right in this locality I know of several substantial beds of wintergreen and of peppermint. There are many other possibilities in barks, roots, and gums. At various times there is a definite undersupply

of the raw materials of various essential oils, especially for those manufacturers and pharmacists who prefer natural to synthetic materials.

In fact, whether by catalog and United States mail, or whether by personal contact, there are many opportunities for one who has the initiative and energy to act as agent for the sale and distribution of locally made goods of all kinds. He is even in the position of stimulating the production of many homemade items. And do not forget that homemade items, if they are good, have a peculiar salability. They carry with them a special flavor of the countryside which produced them, a flavor which, properly presented, has an irresistible appeal to the city consumer.

I have listed the above half-dozen possibilities simply because sitting here I can look around me and see the needs to be filled. I have by no means exhausted the list. In fact the ideas that I have are not half as good as the ideas that you may have. The main thing is to have ideas and imagination and to realize that the success of your experiment in country living lies entirely within yourself.

There are many enterprises which may be undertaken in your own kitchen or workshop which will bring in extra cash. In such cases you are the producer, and you can sell your product direct to your customers. Some nationally known food specialties have had their beginnings in small country kitchens, and the possibilities are by no means exhausted. The list of possibilities includes all items that can be packaged and shipped economically, which you can make at home and give just that extra touch of skill and care that will distinguish them from the common run. Pickles, preserves, jellies, jams, any homemade canned product which is first of all good, and which is attractively packaged, can be sold readily; cookies and candies if they have some special merit or are made according to an unusual receipt. Another possibility is in the realm of cured meats, or meat specialties, such as sausage, scrapple, head cheese, hams and bacons. In many parts of the country where home-grown animals can be cured by household methods of smoking and curing, a big market is developing for these products.

There is one other kind of item which I hesitate to mention because of federal food and drug laws that are sometimes applicable and because there have been abuses. I am referring to the packaging and sale of simple but effective home formulas. My aunt used to make a hard ointment in the form of a stick which was composed of I know not what all, but beeswax and turpentine were two of the ingredients I am sure. I know that it was applied many times to me as a youngster, and it certainly worked. My aunt would carefully heat the end of the stick over the lamp chimney and smear some of the softened ointment on a small patch of flannel, and apply it warm to the wound. As I said it seemed to me to be a sovereign cure. If there is any such formula in the possession of your family, whether it be for softening leather, or sweetening a cider barrel, or what not, it may be something that you can package and sell. Be sure, however, that no misrepresentations are made, or that no law controlling the sale and use of such articles is being violated.

Most old-timers in the country are well aware of the reputed properties of ginseng and of the markets available for it. In the past, American Indians used it for medicinal purposes but did not ascribe to it the magical cure-all powers the Chinese believed it to have. As recently as the first decade in this century an export business of nearly two million dollars a year was flourishing in the eastern states where this plant grew in the moist hardwood forests from Quebec to Georgia. Because it is mostly wiped out now, dealers advertise for people to grow it for them for export.

I particularly want to recommend the production and sale of handicrafts. The making of articles for sale out of wool or leather or metals is a very profitable country sideline. In fact in many instances sidelines of this nature have grown to be major occupations. Small manufacturing establishments are springing up all over Vermont, and, indeed, all over the country. In most cases these small plants have grown out of a home handicraft, and in many the major part of the work has continued to be done right in the home. Such enterprises produce a decent income for the proprietor, and they add to the stability and soundness of the economy of the community where they are located.

Besides articles in wood there are a great many knitted items for which there is a constant demand. Mittens, mufflers, socks, sweaters, shawls, dresses. In this case, as in all others, the determining factor between success and failure is the skill and taste with which the articles are made. Knitted articles must be done in good taste, neatly and simply. This work offers an opportunity for one to express one's originality and skill at designing, but from the practical point of view it is better to stick to patterns of accepted worth, or simple modifications of them. In my opinion the old-time local designs are more acceptable to the type of market you are apt to develop than are the commercial ones that are available in various publications. The same thing goes for hooked and braided rugs and the like, including quilts and covers. Another home industry along this line which is being revived is the weaving of woolen tweeds and homespuns. In one instance that I know of here in Vermont an organization was formed to perpetuate the old time arts and crafts. Money was raised and looms were purchased. These looms were let out to any qualified weaver who would take the yarn of the guild and weave it into cloth of their specifications and pattern. The weavers had the use of the loom free and were well paid for their work by the yard. Provisions were made for the instruction of beginners in the art of weaving. Some excellent fabrics were produced, and the supply of cloth was never equal to the demand for it. The shortage of wood during the war stopped this particular project, but it will be revived as soon as yards are available again. I can testify to the excellence of the product, for I have a very handsome jacket made from the Guild cloth. It is a beautifully designed and woven piece of tweed made from native wool.

Metal work is my special province, for I have a small forge and make various articles in wrought iron for sale. Here is another case where the supply has never been equal to the demand. Fire tools, weather vanes, andirons, candle and lamp stands, sconces, and the like are all very much in demand, and any one who can turn out an honest, strong, well designed and executed article of this nature in iron or sheet metal will never have to worry about selling his product. You will never get rich at it, but you can get a good return for your time and labor, and you will have a cash income sufficient for modest country needs.

People moving to the country have had success setting up a small press, and doing job printing. If you have the skill, you can begin a book-binding business, or hire an IBM composer and do the work that will prepare copy for a printer. If you know how to take pictures, you can start a studio or set up a small business making Christmas cards from photographs. Again I say that your imagination is as good as mine in thinking of possibilities.

Those who are lacking in manual skill and dexterity, but have a background of knowledge of books or maps or prints or glass or furniture, may be able to develop a worthwhile part-time occupation dealing in any one or several of these items. Of course there are many different aspects to getting started as a dealer in books or antiques, but it seems to me that a person having the proper background and connections in the city might be able to develop a part-time business along these lines which would be very much worthwhile. Many have done it before, and the sources for objects to sell are certainly not exhausted yet.

So much for selling country products to the city. If you are a salesman there are many possibilities in selling city products to the country. Here the situation is reversed. Instead of your customers being concentrated and easy to contact in numbers, as they are in the city, they are widely scattered over the countryside, and you have to go to them. That is unless you open a store, which is another thing entirely. In the first place there are certain peripatetic salesmen already established in the country scene. There is the Raleigh man and the Watkins man and the Fuller brush man and the fruit tree and berry salesman, and at least one other who seems now to be fading from the rural scene, the lightning-rod salesman. I am not at all sure that these lines do not offer opportunities to the wide-awake and capable salesman from the city who wants to operate in the country, but I am sure that they are operated on a franchise basis, and opportunities open up only as territories are available. I have it in mind though, that there are other opportunities for selling city products to the country. Nevertheless I cannot help but feel that because of the wide dispersion of the potential customers, and because of the fact that country people have less buying power because of their small cash incomes, this field is not as substantial or as attractive, as selling country products to the city. Another drawback to this type of selling is that it would be harder to make a go of it on a part-time basis, and what is even worse, it necessitates being away from home all day, and possibly for several days at a time. However there is a field, and the possibilities are only limited by your own enterprise and imagination. The list of articles that might be sold could be as long as you wish: household appliances, farm equipment, insurance, and so forth. If you are good at selling and are willing to work at it, you will be able to make a go of it. The product you choose to sell must be one that you know, and one that builds up good will whenever purchased. Do not forget, however, that country folk are aloof to strangers. At least they are in this part of the country. Once you have got a customer, and he is satisfied that he can trust you and depend upon what you say, he will stick with you until the last horn blows, but you will have the devil's own time in breaking the ice and in getting a start.

The basic building trades

An important part of the basic equipment of any farmer is the ability to use his hands. A man who lives out in the country should be able to cope with minor repairs from plumbing to blacksmithing, and he should have the tools and equipment to work with. Further, he should be able to lay out and plan the carpentry and masonry involved in a major building operation, and he should be able to carry on, except in the case of major jobs, with a minimum of outside help. In spite of a widespread ability among farmers to take care of many of their own building needs, there is also work for skilled men in the building trades in the country, and anyone who has talents and experience along these lines will find himself in a position to make an income and live profitably in the country. There are barns, houses, schools to be built and dozens of repair and remodeling jobs to be done.

In the country the building trades are rarely unionized, and in many places there are no building codes. More often than not the type of work to be done is relatively rough and simple, or it is a question of helping someone put together a modular or pre-fabricated building. There are no skyscrapers or apartment houses or mansions to be built, no ornamental plaster work to be done, no imported woods to be worked into trim, no marble tiling to be laid; nothing is required of the workman but simple, straightforward, honest work. The country builder is occupied with repairing existing buildings, altering them and building extensions to them, with occasionally a new wing or barn or outbuilding to construct. For these reasons almost anyone who is willing to work and has some interest in the building trades and has some skill with his hands, will find work to do. The principal requirements are experience and a kit of tools. Experience also can be gained while working as a helper or a laborer for a while, and the tools can be collected over a period of time without too much expense, especially if you are willing to go to country auctions, trading posts and second-hand stores.

I do not mean to inspire unwarranted enthusiasms, but I do know that the demand for workers exists, and that in the city false pride and artificial values, and regulation and unionization, keep many from making a living working with their hands. In fact there are many living in the city now, working at some desk or white-collar job, whose real talents lie in the direction of carpentry or masonry, or plumbing. The pressures of our system of education, the accepted values of our civilization, the weight of public opinion, all tend to demean manual labor of any sort. In the country one more nearly approaches normal living, and the real is more apt to outweigh the artificial. In the country you may have an opportunity to put to work that long dormant gift for working with your hands, and what is more, make a living while doing it.

The housing shortage in the United States at the present time is real and serious. Experts predict that it will be years before the problem is fairly met, and years more before we are finally caught up. Though the housing shortage is principally a city problem, there are areas of serious shortage in the country as well. Some farmers who leave their land and their old houses when they sell to new people cannot foresee any other possibility than a mobile home. Others want a new, small house on the edge of the village, where they can live with a comfort and ease they have never known before. With more and more people choosing to buy old houses or build vacation houses in the country, there is a great demand for building and remodeling. In addition, a majority of farm families are living in houses which are in need of repairs, improvements, and occasionally of replacement.

Twenty-five years ago when this book was first written there were figures available on the needs of farm families. At that time it was believed that 34 per cent needed major repairs, 82 per cent needed running water, 69 per cent needed electric lights and 90 per cent needed central heating. The improvements have been widespread and effective since those days, and these figures are outdated now. And a great many people have gained steady employment for making these improvements. But there is still more to be done.

At that time, which was shortly after World War II, there was a shortage of building material. Since then there has been, until very recently, a good supply. Lumber is again getting scarce, but in the country one can get around such shortages, particularly as far as rough lumber is concerned. Speaking as a country builder, I can say that periodically there are critical shortages not only of lumber, but of some plumbing fixtures, masons' materials, except bricks and concrete blocks, and some lines of millwork such as sash and doors. The situation when shortages occur is not easy, but in the country the greatest drawback to building is likely to be the lack of workers. Few arrive from the city, and many native builders leave.

I firmly believe that there are opportunities in the country for willing and capable workers in the building trades. I further believe that it is not necessary to have a union card, nor to have previously been continuously employed as a carpenter in order to come to the country and work as a carpenter. At this very moment in a house close by, there is a chap working installing a canned gas stove. Previously to coming to the country to live he was employed at a white-collar job in the city. The carpenter who works for me as construction boss was at one time a baker in Jersey City. I know a young fellow who is about to be discharged from the army, and who when he is back in civilian life will return to trade as country builder, and he will find plenty of work to do. Before coming to the country he worked at various jobs in the city; one job was with a wholesale meat house. I myself work at masonry and wrought-iron work; years ago I was in the insurance business. Certainly such work is not for everyone no matter how willing or earnest they may be; for some people an inherent lack of co-ordination precludes the possibility of ever becoming skilled mechanics of any sort. There are many people however who are qualified by interest and abilities, and for these people the very real possibility of earning cash while living in the country exists.

The biggest demand among the building trades in the country is for carpenters. A carpenter is expected to be a versatile cuss, able to tackle any job from jacking up a house to putting new sills under it, to the laying of the roof, whatever sort of roofing it may be. Country carpenters for the most part have not served apprenticeships in their trade. They have learned by working for themselves, with other carpenters with more experience and by study. Some, and these are apt to be the most capable, have worked with and for their father, who was a carpenter before them, and from whom they learned the trade and inherited the tools. In the past many of them have migrated to the city where higher wages were to be found. The carpenters' working day in these parts is eight hours, beginning at seven-thirty in the morning in summers, and possibly at eight in the winter. A car or pick-up truck is a necessary part of his equipment, for his jobs are certain to be scattered and he may have to depend upon himself for transportation. His rate of wage varies greatly with locality, and with conditions. Locally a boss in my village in 1946-7 could expect to get $1.00 an hour, and his helper $.85. And this was exactly twice as much as the pay had been ten years previously. Now a head carpenter gets—not the $10 or $12 he might in the city—but $5.00 or $6.00, and his helper a dollar or so less. The demand for carpenters' services is steady, and now there is again a great deal more work to be done than there are carpenters to do it.

As in the case of carpenters there is a great demand for masons. A country mason is expected to work with stones or bricks or cement blocks, and to be able to plaster as well. Anyone in this part of the country who can build a good fireplace and chimney can get all the work that he can take care of. The poor mason is quite likely to be in the position of having bitten off more than he can chew. This is a situation that a good ambitious newcomer can make capital of. The difference between a good mason and an indifferent one, is that the good one will do more work with less effort. In stone work particularly, masonry is an art; the experienced man with uncanny skill will pick up just the right stone from the dozens available, and will place it so that it lies right without a false move or waste effort. I said "experienced"; perhaps that is not the exact word to use, for some, no matter how long they work at it, never master the trick. Masons are a clannish lot, and they will not casually disclose the tricks of their trade, and there are tricks. For instance, there is a right way to lay a brick, both as to top and bottom and right and left. If you like to do stone work and masonry in general and have the gift, you will have a chance to work at it. There are no deep mysteries or dark secrets; all you need is a strong back and tough hands. The best way to get started is to work at it for yourself as much as you can, and then work out as a mason's helper whenever you get the chance.

Plumbing and heating, lumped together for convenience, are perhaps more specialized trades than are either carpentry or masonry, and the need for a background in actual experience at the trade is greater. For many of the simpler installations, however, there is no reason why a skilled amateur cannot do the job. Plumbers are for the most part an urban crew, and usually they set up in business in the larger villages and cities. The country dweller who is involved in construction work will generally find that the artisan most difficult to get hold of is the plumber. And furthermore he is pretty apt to discover that in terms of labor expended he is the most expensive one. The combination of lack of availability and high price, which characterize plumbers in the country, provides a situation which someone might well take advantage of.

The materials used, if sturdy and true, need not be expensive ones. All the fittings and fixtures required for any ordinary installation can usually be bought from one of the large mail-order houses. But there is one point to make. One of the strangleholds that the plumbing fraternity has on the public is that a plumber will not work on a job where the materials are supplied by the owner. He himself must supply the fittings and fixtures and the customer pays him a nice profit on the items. To make the system more impregnable, plumbers' supply houses will only sell to recognized plumbers, so that the mechanically minded individual who has a notion to do some plumbing for himself, will find it difficult to purchase the necessary materials. They can, as I said, be bought from the mail-order houses, and while such a procedure involves one in certain inconveniences, it is ordinarily a satisfactory way of doing business. The tools required by one plying the plumbers trade are more numerous and expensive than in the other building trades, but again these may be acquired gradually and like fixtures, may be purchased very reasonably from the mail-order houses. I know that any person equipped with the minimum of tools and capable of coping with ordinary simple plumbing installations, will be able to earn while living in the country. Because of the scarcity of plumbers, and because of human inertia, there are a great many country jobs to be had practically for the asking.

There is a warning I'd like to add to men in small contracting, plumbing or other trade businesses, especially to young men just getting started. It has been reported that in an area south of where I live, a land boom and fast development area, there have been some frauds and cheatings. A vacationer or developer will contract with a small businessman to build him a house, or put on an addition. The contract calls for the man's paying half what he'll owe when the job is half done, and the second final amount when the job is finished. The first half is paid all right, according to the agreement, and the builder goes on with the job. But at the end the owner concocts some story about the specs not being followed and refuses to pay. When the builder protests, he soon sees what a hopeless situation he is in. He cannot prove one way or another whether he has followed the specs or not, and the man who refused to pay simply says over and over, "Well, sue me." He says this, in fact, trusting that the young or small business contractor or builder will not be able to afford to sue, and hoping that he will settle for less than the proper amount. People with no recourse or help in such a situation often give in and do settle—thus losing, perhaps, up to half their final fee. If you are going into an area where the scalliwags and fast-buck artists have arrived, beware.

Other trades needed in the country would include those of the electrician, the painter, the decorator, the septic tank builder and servicer, the well driller, and of course the mechanical trades connected with automobiles, and appliance repairmen, and the radio and television experts.

In general the same requirements for transportation obtain in all the building trades or related skills. A car is a virtual necessity, for most of the work will be scattered over a wide area. In some cases the head contractor supplies a small truck to take the workers to the place of construction, and if there are a number of men working on one job, there is a chance of picking up a ride to and from work.

There are many other fields which might be developed. I have a neighbor who picks up spare cash doing all kinds of plain and fancy soldering in his home. The list might be made as long as your arm. The point is, not that they be listed, but that anyone skilled in any of the mechanical trades see the possibility of putting these skills to profitable use while living in the country.

Paying guests

IF YOUR INTEREST IN moving to the country is mainly to engage in farming you will naturally be looking for a place in real farming country. Actually many of the rural areas of our country are not particularly well adapted to farming for one reason or another, but they are wonderful places in which to live. High in the cool mountains, by the brooks and lakes and trails, you will find a lovely countryside, ofttimes intimately interspersed with the rich farming lands of the river valleys. This type of countryside, the land of vacationist, the sportsman, the skier, the tourist, offers many opportunities for all-year-around living. In the first place the qualities which attract others to come and spend their vacation time here are yours for all year around. In the next place the communities are apt to be more versatile and interesting. The lure of the land has always existed and in many of these backwoods and mountain hamlets interesting persons who have long since left the frenzies of the city have settled. These people are as yeast in the dough, and add greatly to the community life of their adopted land. Besides this, the influx of summer people adds zest to the local scene, and what is more important perhaps, they bring money with them. In such places there are opportunities for summer camps, tourist homes, ski lodges, and summer boarders. Here then is a real opportunity to sell country living to others in small doses, and to make money and have fun too.

If you want to provide room and meals, without having the visitors living in the house with you, and if you can procure enough capital, you can start a motel. In most parts of the country, however, such places are standardized and have swimming pools, colored TV and all the features you and your guests may want to escape. Better far, then, to follow the suggestions of the natural resources district people and establish a camp ground with sites for fireplaces and a brook or pond for swimming and fishing.

With the increase in auto travel, longer vacations and shorter working hours, increased interest in hunting, fishing, skiing and outdoor living in general, the demand for a place to stay in the country is on the increase.

127

Whether it is for a farm experience, a wilderness experience or for a handy center to go forth from to fish, hunt, ski or hike, the demand is there and so is the opportunity to make the most of it.

Before the days of motel popularity, many country people who lived on the main-traveled roads throughout vacationland found it possible to pick up extra dollars by taking in tourists. Many times they only provided a room, and the demands of overnight guests of this sort are for the most part simple. What is more, there is no need for a great deal of capital outlay to take care of modest requests for a clean, comfortable place to spend the night. If you had an extra bedroom or two, and your place looked neat and attractive, you were all set for the overnight business. In many areas the tourist business is such that accommodations of this sort are still a possibility for the people who wish to rent rooms for overnight. In spite of the many trailer-campers on the road, and the many young people who simply bring along their sleeping bags, there are still some travelers who refuse to pay motel rates and will settle for tourist rooms. It is important that the beds be comfortable and warmly equipped, and that the furnishings be attractive if you are to hope for repeats. In many states, places which advertise themselves as tourists homes are subject to regulation and inspection by the state Board of Health.

Once your shingle is out, and you discover how much business you can expect in a season, you can decide whether or not further expansion is warranted. In the decades of the 'forties and 'fifties there were many who added to their resource of rooms by building cabins, and then after that many who constructed motels. Sometimes they were justified; sometimes not. My advice is to be sure that the demand exists before spending any real amount of money for expansion, and not to indulge in any jerrybuilt or unattractive development. If you want to attract the right kind of people, people of good taste, clean and sober, your development will not be gaudy, neither will it strive to attract by ingenious but cheap and vulgar imitations of other objects than habitations of man. Nor will your construction be of bizarre materials, made to look like something which

they are not. Keep your buildings in sympathy with the surrounding landscape, reflecting simplicity and dignity in their appearance, and you will have a better chance for lasting success. Unobtrusive but attractive buildings, and scrupulous cleanliness are of primary importance.

If on the other hand you are located far away from the main flow of traffic, but near to one of the hiking or riding trails which abound in resort country, you have a chance to cater to another type of clientele. Campers and hikers come out of the verdant and craggy depths of the forests, and down from the peaks of the mountains. When they do, they will be looking for a place where they can get cleaned up, and where perhaps, they can re-stock their pack baskets, or buy a pair of socks. They will like a square meal with all the fixings and they may want some ointment for a blistered heel, or a bottle of fly dope. There is a chance for a modest success in a well-run place of this kind, if located near one of the well-traveled trails in the national parks, the high mountains or near a footpath like the Appalachian Trail. A modest advertisement in the trail guidebook might be of help. Such an establishment could be of real service to campers and hikers if it offered to serve as a mailing or forwarding address and a place where a chap could pick up some clean clothes which he mailed ahead to himself, and leave soiled gear to be mailed back home. There are possibilities here, not comparable to a location on a main traveled highway, but still worth thinking about. What is more important, this kind of service may be much more in tune with the kind of life-style you want in the country than the other suggestions for accommodating the traveling public.

Perhaps your preference would be for running a summer boarding house. The old-fashioned country boarding house has great appeal for many people and properly handled will produce a reasonable amount of additional cash during the summer months. The danger of getting the wrong kind of people is greater than that of not getting anyone. I do not mean this in any snobbish way at all, but that taking people into your home as paying guests means that they will be a part of the family, as it were, eating at the same table, sitting around the same fire in the evening and using the same facilities. Under such conditions it is important that there be a community of interests and tastes if the undertaking is to be a pleasant one for both parties. When you consider the possibility of running a summer boarding house, do not neglect this factor of intimacy. You can have your own privacy and live your life apart from your boarders by making certain arrangements within your home. If this is the case then the question of what kind of guests you are getting need not be a cause for concern, and you can hang out a sign, or advertise or get your guests any way you choose to.

In the old days we had a neighbor, Mrs. Russell, who for many years ran a very successful country boarding house. She was famous for her pies, and for the table she set; her rooms were clean and neat, and she always had more customers than she could accommodate. Her clients were of long standing, and if ever a vacancy occurred by reason of some change in the plans of one of the old-timers, the person or family who filled the place was sure to be a friend of one of her customers. In fact it came to be a sort of a club, and to be a guest of Mrs. Russell was a mark of special distinction in the little village where she ran her place. In this case the family lived apart from the guests, not mingling with them at all.

On the other hand if your arrangements must be such that it will be necessary for family and guests to share the same living quarters, the best solution, if you are going to take paying guests, is to solicit them from among your friends and acquaintances. You can have a country boarding house, but you can reserve your accommodations for friends only. This need not be at all embarrassing. You friends will probably be getting exactly what they want. They would not feel free to come and stay with you if their presence were a burden. Being able to pay the costs of their provender plus a reasonable amount over gives them just what they want, and it is a legitimate source of revenue for you.

Neighbors half a mile to the south of us have done just this sort of a thing, and very successfully too. They only have room for a very few, but there is seldom a time in summer when their spare rooms are not occupied. Another possibility of augmenting your cash income by selling country living to others, is by running some sort of a camp. I say some sort of a camp advisedly, for there are many different kinds of camp set-ups possible. The conventional boys' or girls' camp is generally a summertime occupation for someone who is engaged in some other business, usually teaching, for the balance of the year. These establishments are often somewhat elaborate, and require extensive buildings and large staff. I do not refer to this type of a camp, although I know of several large camps around the country run along conventional lines, the proprietors of which are country people, living in the country the year round.

The type of camp business I have in mind is one I have experienced myself. It can be fitted into all-year-round country living, being only a subordinate part of the whole. My wife ran this kind of informal camp for young children for many years. Originally, back in the 'thirties, there was no cash outlay involved, and such equipment as became part of the camp, was accumulated a little bit at a time out of the earnings of the camp. It never became a large nor an elaborate affair. The camp, its clientele and its equipment just grew. It was not planned for in the beginning, but parents started and then kept right on asking that their children be accepted to come. In a very few years the camp became so well established that with little effort it could have been changed over into a larger conventional type of summer camp, but neither my wife nor I wished to do that. There were various reasons for this, but most important was our desire not to change our accustomed way of life, wherein the camp played a relatively minor part.

We both liked children, and liked to have them around, so that when a friend was advised by her doctor that it would be better for both her and her child if the child could have a change of scene, preferably in the country, my wife suggested that the boy come and stay with us for a while. Later two other children from the same family came for a short visit, and that was the start of the camp. At any rate the kids had a wonderful time and we enjoyed having them, and so the number of children that we had with us in the summer was gradually increased. With the increase in numbers came the necessity for more help and more accommodations, but the basic nature of the camp never changed. Our camp, which had no name, was a place to which children could come and live as though in a big family. They had all the advantages that country living has to offer kids, the fresh mountain air, loads of sunlight, swimming, and exploring, riding, camping out, hiking, hut building and haying. The older ones had a chance to camp out and cook their own meals, and all of them had some simple household chores to perform. A certain amount of supervision was necessary, to be sure, but there was no rigid regime, and the whole atmosphere at our camp was kept as informal as possible.

The number was limited to twenty, and there were three different places where they slept. They all ate meals together, however. In the little once-abandoned village of Landgrove we retained two houses, one of which is our house and the other house adjacent the one which in summer we used as the camp house. Some of the children slept in the house with us; others in the camp house; others in a rustic cabin on the bank of our stream in the woods. This cabin accommodates seven boys and a counselor. Those living here got their own breakfast, but ate the rest of their meals at the camp house with the others.

Since the camp started with just a few, and outgrew our own house, we had to make some changes in the one we called the camp house. All these improvements, as I said before, were paid for out of the earnings of the camp. The cabin down by the river was built in a spruce grove on the bank of the stream just a little way from the village. It was built by ourselves for the most part, and out of materials growing on the spot. All the framing materials were cut in the woods: the sills, the floor joists, the studs, and the rafters. The stones for the fireplace and chimney were got from the stream. The interior finish is the peeled spruce and plain pine boards. The only purchased materials are the floor boards, the siding, the roof boards and the roofing. The outside finish is of unpeeled softwood slabs, which were had from the mill for the asking. Equipment in the way of cots and mattresses and bedding were acquired gradually as the need demanded, and purchased with the earnings of the camp. The running of the camp has required the services of four or five besides the members of our own family.

I have gone into some detail in describing this camp, because it was a going concern, one that I have first-hand information about, and one which, while bringing in an appreciable contribution to the family income, had not required any large outlay of capital. The cost of the camp house, which was part of our original investment and was not considered at the time for use as a camp house was fifteen hundred dollars.

Many more interesting things could be related about the camp and its activities: The country dances, the art classes, the music, even the rifle range, where all of the older ones learn to shoot. The ages ranged from five to twelve, and there were both boys and girls. But these details, as interesting as they may be, are not the point. Here is a concrete example of what can be done in the way of a summer camp, as an adjunct to country living. There are many more examples if one should search them out, and what is more, I have no doubt that there are other still unexploited possibilities along these lines.

This type of informal camp, requiring relatively little in the way of buildings and equipment, is capable of being modified to suit the tastes and talents of the persons involved. From our experience here I do not hesitate to say that qualified persons could successfully run a tutoring camp along these lines. Speaking from experience with children at our camp and knowing their interest in music, I recommended once and I recommend still that the right persons with proper equipment could fill a real need by running a music camp. It is gratifying to know that a good many such camps were started. It is also gratifying to know that many winter schools in the country have been started along the lines of our summer camp. There must be other possibilities; if this type of undertaking interests you, study it, perhaps you will discover a way of putting to profitable use some special talents that you may have.

Where the climate and terrain is right, there are many opportunities for providing room and board for the winter-sports enthusiasts, especially the skiers. Though in some ski resorts the people who come seem to believe they must have a place to live that provides all the electrical gadgets and washing machines and dishwashers that they would expect to find at home, there are still people who prefer much simpler quarters. At the time I first wrote this book there was a shortage of winter quarters to take care of the skiers who had begun to arrive in such numbers. Since then, in Vermont as well as in Colorado and other western resorts, many have found that if properly located, they can be sure of all the customers that they can handle.

The taking in of paying guests in the winter is a doubly welcome cash sideline for the country dweller, because it will bring in cash at that time of the year when country cash income is at its lowest ebb. It also brings excitement and zest to a season which otherwise might be lonesome and boring. Again I feel qualified to speak, within our geographic limitations, for my wife and I have run a ski lodge, and I have been connected with skiing in varying capacities for several years. At the present time, the camp house next door is used for housing skiers during week ends in the winter, and our son is a qualified professional ski instructor.

Though skiing was already established in New Hampshire and in other towns such as Woodstock and Stowe in Vermont, in our area it did not get started until 1935. In that year the United States Forest service, under the guidance of the Regional Forester and two or three qualified members of the Manchester Winter Sports Club, laid out and cut a ski run through the newly acquired Green Mountain National Forest down the side of Bromley Mountain. The run was immediately a great success and hordes of hardy skiers thought nothing of hiking two and a half miles up hill over the Long Trail, in from Route 11 to get to the bottom of the upper section of the Bromley Run. From there it was a semi-vertical mile up the run to the top of the mountain; half an hour of laborious side-stepping and herring-boning up through the winter forest, the reward, five minutes of breathtaking, terrifying, exhilarating descent. Seeing the numerous cars parked at the foot of the trail and realizing that there were no facilities of any sort near the spot we bought a piece of land on the highway at the junction of the Long Trail. The property included a jerrybuilt and dilapidated filling station and road stand. We junked the filling station, and during the next summer remodeled and rebuilt the old building. Bricks for the six-foot fireplace were hauled down the Long Trail by hand from one of the old charcoal kilns up on the mountain. Wide native pine was obtained from a nearby mill for the interior finish, and central heating and plumbing were installed. The entire operation was on a strictly shoe-string basis, but somehow it was managed. The following winter we were ready for our guests by the time the first snow fell, and we were all set to operate the first ski lodge in our part of the country.

It proved to be an interesting and exciting and profitable winter. We had a hectic time of it for three days over the week ends, with a minimum of eighteen hours of hard work each of these days, and then four days in the middle of the week to recuperate. We met many interesting people, and made lasting friendships. We had sleeping accommodations for sixteen people, three small bunk rooms with two double tiers of bunks, and two de luxe rooms with only one lower and one upper each. We had two tiny bath rooms each with a shower. We had our own living quarters just off the most important room in the house, the kitchen. Besides this we had a large living room, about twenty by forty, and along one side of this room, which had a great fireplace in one end, was a dining alcove, with room for about eight four-place tables. More often than otherwise on week ends hungry diners overflowed the chairs and tables, and the floor of the living room was covered with skiers gratefully eating the wonderful food my wife served. In that little place we served as many as one hundred and fifty dinners at one meal. Our rates were low, we charged three dollars and a half for room and three square meals, for we were primarily interested in college kids and youngsters who could not afford high prices.

In spite of our modest prices and good food we enjoyed a profitable and exciting winter. Moreover, during the week in the lull between the frenzied weekends, we all had a chance to ski to our hearts' desire.

This extremely interesting and profitable enterprise came to an end for two good reasons. The first and most decisive was that in the late summer of the next year, our ski lodge burned to the ground, together with everything that was in it. The other reason, and the reason we never rebuilt, was that the place was located about nine miles away from our home, and it was not practicable to keep both places going. We could not satisfactorily divide our interests. We had to decide which place we were going to live in, and there was more to keep us here at home, so we never rebuilt.

Out of this experience developed several conclusions as to skiers and the business of caring for them. As a group skiers are the easiest people to take care of that could be expected. Searching for an explanation of this, I think it is found in the nature of the sport itself. Otto Schneibs, famous ski authority and instructor, who by the way, was one of the many interesting guests at our ski lodge, says "Skiing is not merely a sport—it is a way of life." In the preface to Schneibs book *Skiing for All,* Eugene Du Bois wrote, "Skiing brings man closer to earth—takes us further from the sordidness of work and war—than any other sport. Skiers need not confine themselves to man-made trucks, the channels and the stadia of other games. Skiers know only the limitations of nature's snow—her trees—her rocks—her insurmountable altitudes." It is the demand that skiing makes on its devotees, this demand for ruggedness and fortitude, that set them apart from all others from the innkeeper's point of view. This, and the fact that the major interest in skiing is in the sport itself, and not in its trappings, seem to be the reasons for the skiers' good nature and grateful response toward any efforts made for them. They are however a boisterous and noisy lot. Their caps and mittens, and jackets and socks and boots are always wet, and as soon as they shed them, which is as soon as they come in the house, they are dumped in a wet messy heap, all over the place. They track in snow, they clump around in their heavy ski boots, they talk loudly and all at once concerning their experiences on the trails and slopes, they sing all over the place, and some of them even play musical instruments of one sort or another which they bring along with them. It might even be said that, when, after a day in the open, subjected to the sub-zero winds of the mountain tops, they are gathered around the fire drinking their tea laced with rum, or their hot grog, or their Tom and Jerries, some of them imbibe a bit too freely. Then, too, there is the problem of drying their gear, and storing their skiis, and also, in the old days, of waxing their skis, usually done indoors where it was warm. Nowadays the only serious waxers are the cross-country skiers, who prepare for up and down hill, in all sorts of weather and snow conditions, on their light wooden skis. This new interest among the young ecology-minded skiers is an innovation that fits in with other concerns of the young. The sense of freedom from the conventional ski-tow is obviously one of the appeals to these youths.

Of course you cannot expect people to come to ski unless there is snow—natural or man-made. At the beginning of the ski craze, if it may be called that, many mistakes were made which would be less likely today. Some ski developments were undertaken on the basis of insufficient information as to snow conditions. People made the mistake of embarking on enterprises involving the outlay of too much money in relation to the snow probabilities. One or two exceptional winters misled them, and they entered ventures not justified over the years. Now that there can be man-made snow, if you can afford to support it, such failures are less likely.

Still, the skiing season is a relatively short one, and it is difficult to set up a hostelry or inn on the basis of the ski trade exclusively unless there are other attractions to bring tourists in the summer as well. But if you are in the snow belt, and if you are near the facilities that skiers demand, and if you can regard the ski business as an adjunct to other enterprises, you are all set to pick up some useful cash in the winter time, and to have a lot of fun as well. Feed your skiers well, and you will probably succeed.

In conclusion, I want to quote from a publication of the United States Forest Service. It seems to me to be significant and helpful for all who want to cater to people seeking recreation in the forests and field, on the lakes and streams and in the country in general.

"Today, Americans in general exhibit a restless interest in forest hunting, fishing, camping, picnicking, nonprofessional collecting, riding, swimming, boating, exploring the wilderness, cross-country skiing, snowshoeing, and auto touring....All these forms of recreation when practiced in the forest, have common characteristics. Like the forest they are in sharp outward contrast to the usual environments of life—as different from them as the electric stove in the steam-heated city apartment is from the open campfire at the edge of the lake. They have the inner aspects of naturalness, freshness, simplicity, cleanliness, and a more or less primitive quality, in equally sharp contrast to the artificiality, monotony, elaborateness, and sophistication of the city.

"All these things belong to the forest. They are in tone with it and inseparable from it. They remove man from the dominance of artificial patterns and schedules and bring relaxation and leisure. There he need encounter no time clocks to punch, no trains to catch, no jostling, no elbowing, no narrow walls and foetid air, no split-second dashing from one pressure task to the next. Humans may seek adventure in their own way, and on their own terms—hunt, shin up a mountain, or loaf—and thereby capture a sense of freedom personally. They are removed from the necessity to meet business engagements, to keep books, to write letters, to tend a machine, to keep house. They can live for the moment on their own. They can wear clothes of their choice, eat when they please, loaf or work, go exploring, or to go sleep undisturbed. They may catch the largest fish, build the best camp fire, bake the tastiest Dutch oven bread, climb the highest mountain, or discover the most breathtaking view. They have the chance to regain physical and mental tone; to achieve satisfying, wholly personal proof of their abilities and prowess; to recapture a sense of their own personal significance, and to rest."

Small workshops
and small plants

T HIS IS THE DAY of opportunity for small plants in the country. A small plant by my definition is any enterprise which, because of the nature of the work done, requires a separate building to house its machinery and operations and one which requires the employment of one or several or up to about ten or twelve people working as a group or as a family. I realize that to many this will seem to be a super small plant, but I have so defined it, for I am interested in one-man or one-family operations which do not require a great outlay of capital. This book is not addressed to industrialists, and no part of its theme is devoted to the decentralization of industry. I am interested in a discussion of how country living may be possible for persons now living in the cities, and small one-man or one-family plants are extremely important in that discussion. This for several reasons: first, because I am convinced that there are great opportunities along these lines; because I see around me several very successful exploitations of the small plant idea, and because I run one myself.

To my way of thinking there is a fundamental difference between a small plant and a home industry. This is because a small plant cannot properly be housed in the home, and it differs from the conventional industrial set-up in that there is no plan or desire for expansion beyond certain well-defined limits. The small plant is properly the outgrowth of a home workshop, and is concerned with turning out a product which is beautiful, imaginative, useful and in good taste. There is no aim to compete with articles manufactured on a large scale by production-line methods. Where a large family or commune has plenty of room, a small plant can, of course, be operated right there in the family's living quarters.

Small plants are justified because there is a demand for their products, a demand which can be translated into a reasonable return for the labor of those who run the plants. The demand exists because there are people in the world who want and are able to pay for simply designed and honestly made articles such as can only be supplied by the type of plant that I am talking about. The mechanized and production-line methods of large plants and factories cannot produce these articles, and they never will be

141

able to produce them. There is no doubt but that they can produce similiar articles, and a very good chance that the article which they produce will be the cheaper of the two although that does not necessarily follow.

The type of plant I have in mind will use hand labor, but it will also use machines, to be sure, if machines will help to produce economically and conveniently; it will use the best and most effective and up-to-date methods possible, but a good bit of the work will necessarily be hand work. The advantage that such plants enjoy over larger and more mechanized plants is that the method and process of production will be under the personal supervision of the proprietor, and the construction and design of the article will be determined by utility and good taste. In every case the care and skill of the operator will be recognizable in the product itself. Low overhead and ideal living conditions and personal relations between employer and employee are factors which operate favorably for the proprietor in producing his goods economically. Most important of all, however, is the fact that here is a chance to produce something and to have intimate and personal pride in the object produced. To make the best thing of its kind that can be made is the prime mover.

With a small plant the profit motive as such is not to be considered. The owner or group who runs the small plant will try to obtain a decent and fair return on the labor and investment involved, but there are no stockholders to be satisfied. The lack of that profit motive is the principal reason that a small plant must and will remain small. As soon as the profit motive urges one on to expansion beyond the limits of personal supervision the whole character of the enterprise is changed and the personalized plant which was a stabilizing influence in the normal life of the community, and brought a decent living to its proprietor, disappears in the industry which engulfs the community and brings worry and possible riches to the owners.

As I said, normally such a plant as I have described will gradually evolve from the home workshop, but not necessarily. Just as a newcomer to country living can buy and equip a farm, and then run it, learning as he goes along, paying for his mistakes, so can a person with a sound idea and adequate capital, start a small plant from scratch, or buy up a small plant already in operation. In either case, however, it is preferable if there is a certain amount of experience and skill to go along with the enthusiasm and capital. It is also preferable that the beginnings be on an extremely modest scale, for the ideal plant layout can only be achieved by trial and error, and the operator and his apprentices are much better off learning together on a small scale first.

I fall back on my own personal experience to illustrate my point. When I was a kid spending my summer vacations on my uncle's farm, the most fascinating spot of all was the forge which he had in one corner of his workshop. Here my uncle made repairs to his farm machinery, and did odd jobs of smithing for his neighbors. Under his capable and tolerant guidance I learned how to light and care for my fire, what the various guidance tools were for and how to use them, and here I made my first attempts at forging iron and steel. The fascination that forging held for me, and my interest in it never left me, and when we finally left the city and came to the country some twenty years after those youthful efforts, I found myself in a position where I could set up my own forge. My first forge was a decrepit riveter's forge about the size of a frying pan, which I found in one of the buildings on the place, and my first anvil was a broken-faced cast-iron one which I picked up in some farmer's scrap pile. I collected a hammer or two, a few makeshift pairs of tongs, and set up my shop in one corner of one of the outbuildings on the place.

Here I messed away at odd moments for some time, gradually acquiring some knack, and becoming more interested all the while. Soon I had a chance to pick up a larger portable forge at second hand, and a better anvil, still battered and worn, but at least steel-faced. By now I was actually making things, and, in fact, made H and HL hinges for use in our home which we were remodeling at the time. These hinges are still in use, but I never draw anyone's attention to the fact, nor do I point them out with pride. In the meanwhile by virtue of attendance at auction sales and snooping around all the blacksmiths' shops that I could go into, I had acquired a workable stock of forging tools and tongs, and had bought a modest stock of flats and rounds and squares in mild steel.

Without going too much into detail, I can say that again I outgrew my equipment and my location as well, so that I remodeled another small outbuilding on the place, built in a proper forge, bought a new Swedish steel anvil, laid in a stock of Norway iron, and moved into my new location. Up to this time my activities had been more or less of the nature of a spare-time hobby, but now with a proper forge with a good blower, a new anvil, and real wrought iron to work with, I began making things for sale, as well as taking on such repair work as the neighboring farmers brought in to me.

I added copper and tin and sheet iron to my stock of raw materials and made weather vanes and wall sconces, and various sheet-metal objects as well as the work in wrought iron. As it was difficult to procure the sort of stuff that I was now equipped to make in my shop, I began to get orders from architects for all sorts of special hardware and fittings. I copied old thumb-latch sets for use in houses that were being remodeled, I did the hardware for entire houses, I did special lamps and lighting fixtures, and in one instance made a copper dove of peace with an olive branch in its mouth to go on the top of a church steeple. After that, ironically enough, I went to war.

When I came back, I decided to start a small plant and pick up where I left off and go on. I began to make more of my iron work than ever before. Since my old shop was dark, without enough clearance overhead, and impossible to work in during the winter because of the cold, I built a new building, designed expressly for the purposes to which it was to be put. The lay-out and design are a result of experience gained from the shortcomings of the two previous shops.

I do not mean to give the impression that the above is the only way, or even the best way, in which a small-plant industry is to be started. Anyone who has worked at some specialty either professionally or as a hobby, while living in the city, may have just the proper background and experience for setting up a small shop in the country. The city basement workshop or laboratory may have developed all the experience necessary. The city kitchen might well be included, for small plants located in the country can be devoted to the making of food products or specialties as well as anything else.

One other gratifying way to get started with a small plant is to buy up and bring back a plant already established and equipped, but no longer operating. Woodcraft shops in our area have been brought back as have several other kinds of establishments.

Again I want to say that I am sure that the opportunities for small plant operations in the country are good. The experience of my friend Vrest Orton in Weston, Vt., with his country store, and of the dozens who have imitated him, has definitely established the fact that the demand for the type of article you can make in a small plant is in excess of the supply. Though any such shops now mix imported articles in with their stock of articles made nearby, there is a very real sales advantage for the small producer in the country, just by virtue of his being a small producer in the country. Now that there is such a volume of traffic from the city to the country, the buyer comes nearly to the producer's door.

Small plants rarely have labor troubles, and certainly no troubles of any size. In many instances the plants can be located strategically as to raw materials. Unless the plant makes spinning wheels or large pieces of furniture, the product is rarely bulky; and this means the added advantage of reduced expense for transit or trucking. The location away from main highways is likely to be more of an advantage than a handicap.

The idea of small plants scattered over the countryside is no visionary's dream, no vaporing from the mind of an impractical romantic. There are many such plants now in successful operation, a number of which I am personally familiar with. There are surely many more of them up and down the broad expanse of our country which have yet to be brought to my attention. And what is more important, so I sincerely believe, is that markets are not glutted and that there is room for many more enterprises of this sort.

Where there is a good supply of wood, or where it is possible to procure wood at reasonable cost, for the man who enjoys woodcraft there is an excellent opportunity. Near me is the Red House Workshop which started as a home workshop enterprise supplying the Vermont Country Store. The articles produced from native woods are original in design and of sound workmanship, decorated with skill and taste, and there came to be a steady demand for the entire output of the plant. Products that can be made in such a small plant include bowls, some kinds of baskets, small pieces of furniture, wooden mobiles, spinners' and weavers' equipment, flower tubs, hat racks and a hundred others. Your imagination can dictate what you will do.

For example, you can make toys. In a few towns away from Landgrove there is a craftsman who makes extraordinary rocking-horses, in a class by themselves. They are sold to the quality trade in New York. Another plant I'know of makes children's play pens; another makes toy trains of wood, the engineer of which bobs up and down in his cab as the train rolls along. There has recently been established on a main road down in the valley in a little settlement of craft shops a store called "The Enchanted Dollhouse," which sells every imaginable sort of doll—wooden and otherwise—as well as every sort of dollhouse. Blocks are easy to make and appealing to children, especially if there are shapes included which fire their imagination. Many kinds of creative and educational toys have a good market, and I believe there is not an adequate supply of quality goods of this sort to supply the demand for them.

A cheese factory is a possibility for those living in the right place who can acquire the necessary skills. In Vermont there are several small cheese factories which do very well. One, in Healdville, makes cheeses which have been famous for decades, and known wherever gourmets gather. This is the Crowley cheese made in a small plant that is a father-to-son affair, now in its third and fourth generation. Their knowledge and skill are outstanding, and those are the prime requisites, to be sure; but knowledge and skill are not impossible of attainment. The most important factor is the determination to produce a fine cheese, handmade under rigid personal supervision. A Crowley cheese used to be a great favorite at the haunt of newspapermen in New York near Times Square, Bleeck's. In the old days I used to go there quite often, and I found that the great epicure who did a column for *Gourmet* for so many years, and who wrote for the old New York Herald Tribune, Lucius Beebe, was very likely to have a Crowley cheese cached behind the bar at Bleeck's. He kept it there for use at his table when the occasion demanded something special in the way of a cheese.

The proof that others can do somewhat the same thing that the Crowleys have done can be found in several small plants started in dairy country. One friend of mine, Bob Allen, bought up an unused creamery and produced the excellent Londonderry cheese, which found a ready market for all he could produce. In Grafton, a town not far from here, the town fathers built and offered a small cheese factory for use as an aid to local employment, and it has done well, too. Such cheeses are carried by all the gift shops and fine foods stores in the vicinity. They are easy to ship, and are in great demand at Christmas time for gifts.

I know of a man who made cross-country skis and supplemented his income by making garden furniture out of locally obtainable wood. I know another who made fine bowls out of maple wood, and the spoons and forks to go with them. One man north of here makes fine dies and molds used by a local manufacturer of plastics. Another makes picture frames and does picture framing. Pottery shops are becoming common, and so are jewelry, leather work and basket shops. Wrought iron work, as already mentioned, is a possibility as well as such sheet metal items as signs, weathervanes and so forth. And again I would mention printing, photography, bookbinding, home-spun yarns from native fleece and hand-woven tweeds and suitings. Another enterprise which enjoys great success is the candle mill. Many families of young people living together make candles, and derive a good income from it. In the town of Arlington, Vermont, in an old converted barn, an enterprising and generous family has started a mill and display place where people can observe the workers doing all the steps necessary to turn out the many utilitarian and decorative candles produced here.

Such an enterprise, which has enjoyed great success, shows what is perhaps a truism: that he who has imagination and a willingness to work can find a place for success even in the country, particularly if the general trend in the area is toward a recreational economy. The most important sort of small plant, whether it is included in my list of suggestions or not, is the one you already know about—the one you would operate to make the thing you like to make.

The professions

I AM CERTAIN, though, that in comparable categories the countryman has a greater chance for a spontaneous glimpse of the wider horizon than does the city dweller, and it seems to me for the professional man or woman working in the country, the chances are better than for anyone else. I can think of no better reason than this in urging the advantages of country living upon those trained for, or engaged in, the practice of a profession.

Of hope for work to do there is plenty, of hope for great rewards financially there is less certainty. The average old-time countryman spends little for professional services; in many cases they are scarce and inaccessible. Fame and fortune for the professional man who moves to the country may be out of the question, but again we are confronted with a question of values, and that question must be decided by the man who makes the choice. The most I can hope to do is to provoke an honest and searching examination of values. The serenity that comes with the knowledge of work well done, the freedom from exacting professional routine, the lack of abnormal strains and pressures, the joys of the trout streams and the woodcock and grouse covers, all are his who lives and practices in the country. You yourself will have to decide what the good life is, and how badly you want the things that can and cannot be bought with money.

Physicians, lawyers, engineers, teachers and writers have all come to the country to make a new way of life for themselves. In some areas there are shortages that cry to be filled. Many a physician has responded to such shortages, but the need still persists. None of the studies made on country living that I have been able to get my hands on has reported any shortage of lawyers in the country, nor have they reported any rural hardship as the result of lack of legal facilities. The case then, is not the same as with physicians, where a definite shortage does exist; but in spite of this, one wishing to practice law will find many good reasons for picking the country, or rural areas as a place in which to practice and live and bring up his family. Here he will find more frequent glimpses of that "wider horizon," more actual experience with all the various aspects of the legal profession, more intimate contact with people, a wider acquaintance with bench, bar, and state officialdom.

There are probably as many jobs available for an engineer as for members of any of the other professions. I will concede that my experience is pretty much localized; so I say only that in this part of the country there is a lack of enough qualified professional men in surveying, structural work, in sanitation and water-supply work, as well as in some aspects of highway work, to get all the necessary parts of a job done promptly and efficiently. With the new environmental laws there is a crying need in the field of engineering for stream pollution control and sewage disposal.

The problem of the pollution of our streams is a burning one at present, and is a subject which is getting more and more attention from the general public. The time has come when we must see the utter stupidity and folly of turning our streams, with all their recreational and aesthetic possibilities, into open sewers. In the capital city of my own state, the main street upon which the State House fronts is paralleled by a stream which was used for sewage disposal by all the municipalities which line its banks. The result was an ugly, disgusting and noisome situation. In hot weather when the stream is low, and there is little air stirring, the stench from the stream would lie over the city of Montpelier like a miasma. This is what had been done to what could become one of the loveliest streams in the country, the Winooski River, a stream which cuts through the contorted bulk of the Green Mountains between the peaks of Camel's Hump and Mount Mansfield, amid scenes of true grandeur. This kind of thing has been happening in large and small cities throughout the country during the last fifty years. With the new laws, and a new generation of engineers, some of the filth is being cleared up; but a great deal remains to be taken care of. Here is a field that should offer continuous employment until the whole job of cleaning up is done. Working at any of the parts of this job, one could live in the country, whether it be surveying of streams, water testing and study of degrees and causes of pollution, the laying out of new sewers or the construction and design

of treatment plants. One could be enjoying all the benefits of country life and be doing his fellow countrymen a great service while doing it.

At the time this book was first written, the Soil Conservation Service, which was new then, was in need of the services of engineers for their reclamation and drainage work. Now the Natural Resources Conservation Service, its successor, is still in need of engineers for a wider variety of jobs on all the conservation fronts. Here again, a man working for this service would feel that he was contributing significantly to the preservation of country ways of living while working to conserve the farmland, wildlife, natural resources and the countryside in a state necessary to make country living possible at all.

The teaching profession has become filled up in recent years with young people wanting to move to the country. As already stated in an earlier chapter, some rural states are nearly swamped with applications from teachers wishing to move out of the cities, or from young teachers just out of college or graduate training who want to begin their careers in the country. From what I can gather, both private and public schools are experiencing the same pressures.

Though exceptions are sometimes made, ordinarily a person wishing to teach should have completed a prescribed course in a Normal School or Teachers' Training College, or have bachelor's or master's degrees with a major in education. State certificate requirements vary, but those applicants that meet the state requirements are of course given priority when the officials make their choice of candidates. This situation automatically closes the doors on the average person who wishes to live in the country and to make such living possible by teaching in a rural public school. Obvious qualifications, or experience of teaching in a private school will not help. This is a great pity, for unless a person can locate a job in a private school, the many talented people thinking of coming to the country to teach are shut off as a rule from public school teaching, both to their own disadvantage and to the disadvantage of rural education. In any case, it would be worthwhile for one interested in teaching in rural schools as a means of making a living while living in the country, to check with the State Board of Education of any state in which he is particularly interested.

Teaching in private schools is another matter entirely. Persons qualified by background and character and education may be able to find a place with some private school in the country, but the field is very limited.

There are teaching possibilities other than teaching in schools public or private. Some of these have been mentioned earlier in connection with camps, but they need not necessarily be an adjunct to camping. Tutoring and music lessons both offer a chance to pick up some extra money. Many arts and crafts can be taught. In fact, if you have a talent, there is very likely to be someone around who wants you to teach it to him—be it how to build musical instruments, how to make vegetable dyes and to dye wool, make candles, make furniture or even cook, preserve, sew or increase your speed of reading.

Stenography, auditing, bookkeeping, designing houses or shopping centers, editing and proofreading can all be professions carried on in the country.

One kind of job necessarily done in the country is in the growing field of forest conservation work. Young people looking toward a future life in the country might well plan their education to prepare them for a job with the United States Forest Service, with a wildlife commission, a fish and game department, with the Department of Agriculture's Extension Service or with various state forest services. In addition to those government jobs, there are forest foundations of one sort or another offering conservation work, and there are paper and lumber companies, both large and small, which need forestry specialists.

Some jobs in these fields are open to untrained people, but the chances for advancement are small. Both the National Forest Service and the National Parks Service can take untrained people, though trained personnel is their greatest need. Candidates should be specially fitted for work outdoors, should have a great love of the outdoors, and have vision and the competence to turn that vision into reality. Much important work is neglected in our national forests when unsufficient trained help is available. Job requirements both for federal jobs and state jobs with forestry or park services can be had for the asking.

From the standpoint of creative work there is nothing to equal living and working in the country. Scott and Helen Nearing, who used to live in Jamaica, Vermont, and whom I visited during the winter of 1972 in Maine, have proven to the thousands who have read their book *Living the Good Life* that the two are totally compatible.

My guess is that they moved away, not because of the pressures of the ski development on Stratton Mountain, which had not been started at that time, but because by now the world had beaten a path to their door and they found little of that solitude, the longing for which caused them to move to Vermont in the first place.

By now their maple syrup had prospered, and there were several new buildings on the land. There were living quarters in these buildings, and they were seldom unoccupied, for a great and generous hospitality spread out from the stone house which Scott and Helen had built with their own hands. At any rate there were people around at all times of the year; and while each one of these visitors, mostly strangers, pulled their oar, no doubt there must have been little time for the music and reading and writing which made up the life that the Nearings craved.

Ever since I had met Scott when he first came to the farm in Jamaica and before he moved there to live, I felt a deep respect and admiration for this man (and later for his wife) and while we did not see each other very often, their leaving left a hole in my life. All the time down through the years since they left, I felt a strong pull tugging away at me to go see them (they had been here) and here at last I found myself on their threshold in Maine.

To put it mildly, I was glad I went, and will be eternally grateful to the two nice people who drove me there. We had left Landgrove betimes and then spent the night in Wiscassett, from whence we reached the

Nearing homestead before lunch. I received a warm welcome from Scott and was introduced to the young man who turned out to be a pilgrim, as I was, who had driven up from central Massachusetts just for a visit with the Nearings.

Then Helen burst from the kitchen door and with a hug and a kiss I was given a welcome which was truly a blessing. It was an event that my spirit was sadly in need of. Then Helen and my friends went in out of the bright sunshine and left Scott and Bob to finish the task they had undertaken.

It was a nice room, that kitchen, with a nice smell; and there was a pot of soup, among other things, on a woodburning stove, which was a Home Comfort, I believe. Helen told me it was the kind she had wanted, for modern times had clothed even woodburning stoves in white enamel, leaving one to suppose that old-fashioned stove blacking was not to be endured.

Leading off the kitchen was a large low-ceilinged living room with a stone fireplace. This had been temporarily stopped up, making way for an old-fashioned woodburning stove which was crackling away. This was all of the house I saw except for the music room with its large two manual keyboard organ; and with Helen's violins beneath it.

The living-room windows looked across a small pond, which was completely hidden under the snow, up a gentle slope beyond to the edge of the ever-present wall of fir trees. Here at their edge was a woodshed which fitted into the scene; and several tepees of fir trunks which had been stacked thus so that they would dry. The garden was below on the other side of the house, and we saw little of it other than the stone retaining wall which separated it from the house yard.

But to tell the truth, I was so involved with the people and with our excited exchange of catching up with each other, that I did not pay my usual careful attention to my surroundings. All I can report is that both inside and out here was a pleasant and comfortable place which showed at every turn the love that had been expended on it. Now Scott and Bob came in; and in due course a long stretcher table as pulled out from the wall, and we all sat down while Helen proceeded to put the vegetarian meal on the table.

At this point I might interject that, in view of their experiences at Jamaica, there were no provisions made at this place for anyone to stay overnight. Thus the pilgrims, and if I remember correctly, Helen said there were nearly 1,800 of them last year, come, satisfy their curiosity and then leave on the same day they came. Even at that, I could not help but wonder how, with that many people tracking in over the remote roads, the Nearings could get anything done.

Nevertheless they do get a great deal done, for they build houses, write many books, make music, and spend some though not a great deal of time preparing their excellent vegetarian meals. As they describe in *Living the Good Life,* their schedule for physical work and intellectual work is very precisely planned and carried out. They have worked out for themselves a way of country life that was eminently satisfactory for them and, though austere, it has become an ideal for the hundreds who have read their book about their country style of life with such deep interest and desire for emulation today.

Country living has also become a goal for many artists in spite of their strong tendency for gathering together in groups in the great capitals of the world. Groups are stimulating, especially for those engaged in creative work of one sort of another, and with the cars and good roads we have today artists who live in the country are not so remote from one another as they might have been in the past.

It is worth noting, however, that group movements often can bear a depressing resemblance to cults and fads. Artists' colonies tend to dissipate one's time and energy in a hectic whirl of conversation and conviviality. The seeking for kindred spirits is more apt to be a result of lack of self-sufficiency than it is to be a mark of genius. Of the need that some personalities seem to have for the hurly-burly of metropolitan life there can no doubt; one can hardly imagine Balzac outside of Paris, or

Dickens outside of London, but to assume that in order to do creative work in the arts one must live amid the noise and odors and distractions of a great city is to fall into serious error.

It is true that the artist and the writer find that for the most part the markets for his wares lie in the big cities; here are the museums, the art galleries, the collectors; here are the literary agents, the editors, the publishers; but except in the case of certain special types of work the necessity for being close to one's market no longer exists. The proof that this is so lies in the increasing numbers of artists who are living and working in the country. I do not mean to imply that I am a writer or that my friend is an artist, but it is worth noting perhaps that as I sit here in the office of my blacksmith shop pecking away at the typewriter, my friend is painting just behind my back, trying to catch the glory of the snow-covered hillside across the frozen stream. The western sun is brilliant on the white birches and evergreens, the snow has a rosy glow from the sun itself, the trees and the shadows make a pattern against the snow, and the sky is blue beyond description.

The advantages that country living has to offer to the artist and to the writer are many, and self-evident. Not the least of these is that it is less expensive to live in the country than in the city. In addition to this, the artist or the writer enjoys the great advantage of being employed at a type of work that does not tie him down, nor does it bind him to any one given locality. In the past perhaps, a man engaged in commercial art work had to be close to his market in order to get the job, but this is becoming less and less the case. Moreover, because of the fact that great many people engaged in creative work have come to the country to live, it is possible to have stimulating contacts and to have a quiet and serene existence at the same time. In addition to these are the joys inherent in living in the country. All who look to the country with the hope that there they may find a way to lead a normal and satisfying life have some inkling of what these joys may be, but in almost every case in which the dream becomes a reality, the realization is greater than was the anticipation.

Reflections

THAT IN GENERAL throughout the world the condition of man is worsening in a frightful manner, many will deny, but these are the congenital self-deceivers, the rationalizers, those who find it more acceptable to cherish an untruth than to face the facts. It is comforting to think as did Dr. Pangloss that everything is for the best....or could be if only the system were changed. But those who scorn not the reading and the record of history are aware of the fact that the story of man is not one of steady and uninterrupted rise from the primordial ooze to the musical and philosophical profundities of the Beatles.

He who detects and defines some of the illusions feels at times he must speak out. If we in America are on the wrong track—and this seems to be the case—it is necessary that we attempt to find out how and why. If we admit we are on the wrong track, it follows logically that we are accepting as true something less than the truth.

There are twelve fallacies that we all too often take for truths: the first is that we think that as far as humans are concerned inheritance does not significantly weigh as a factor in a person's condition in life; the second is that environment results in the debasement of man, not that debased man produces the debased environment; third, that with human beings, differences between physical attributes have no corresponding differences between attributes that are not physical.

In addition to these three there are the fallacious conceptions that change represents progression, and that the latest moment in time is the point of furtherest progress; that there are no desirable values which cannot be measured physically or evaluated numerically in material terms; that social inequities can be eliminated if only the proper political or social formulae be applied; and that science will be able to repair any damage to man's environment which has resulted from mechanization or technological development.

The eighth fallacy is that aggrandizement is universally desirable, whether it be manifest in the Gross National Product, miles per hour, population, or in the years of a man's life. That the individual cannot be held responsible for his acts—the responsibility lies with society; that the debasement of man results from the evils of society, all men having been born good and pure; that atomic weapons are merely more powerful weapons, like a bigger and better Big Bertha over the catapult, and not a whole new thing altogether.

Perhaps most important, is the mistaken idea that a soft mind is the equivalent of a tender heart; as Candide said, our "optimism is the madness of maintaining that everything is right when it is wrong."

Fallacy number nine, which is certainly a premise which all of our Federal Government, our transportation experts, medical science and all the real estate high-pressure promoters have accepted, reveals itself as an enormous error as soon as it is rigorously scrutinized.

Some believe that new industry means creating a better place to live. I say: New industry does not necessarily result in an increase in prosperity. More often, industrialization leads to increased taxes and municipal indebtedness, and in the destruction of the environment.

Thirty years ago I wrote a modest little treatise on vegetable gardening. At the time I had not the courage to dispute the authorities, and while I did not practice the techniques promulgated by the U.S. Department of Agriculture and its infinite offshoots operating out of the land-grant colleges and elsewhere, I pussyfooted along with their accepted dogma.

As an example of what I mean, I devoted space to a description of the chemical fertilizers and insecticides, even though I did not use them myself. I accepted them but soon discovered that one did not need them. After 16 additional years of vegetable growing experience, it became apparent how mistaken the practices of chemical gardening were, and I was no longer willing to have my tacit acceptance stand, so I wrote another book.

This book pointed out the dangers of the use of chemicals, either as plant foods or as insecticides or herbicides. While I proposed no solution for the dilemma with which commercial growers now find themselves faced, I did point out that the home gardener was infinitely better off without the use of chemicals, and fully described alternate means of producing luxuriant growth. For my pains I was described as a fanatic, and the book, in spite of the fact that it is a good one, fizzled out. It has since been re-issued by Rodale Press as *Step-By-Step To Organic Vegetable Growing.*

The thing that has disappointed me most is that it seems impossible to get those who scorn the organic method to come and look at the results. Here is a refusal to recognize the truth by the simple, stupid and disastrous means of turning one's back on the evidence. Being a professional gardener, I look at all gardens within my reach, and recently had the opportunity for the close examination of several carefully tended backyard gardens in Montpelier, where home garden rivalry runs high, and not even the very best of them showed the growth and perfection that can be seem here in my garden where climatic conditions are more unfavorable than in most places.

So it goes: all who see it admire it and exclaim at its beauty and perfection, but where are the ones who scorn the methods? Those who insist that it is impossible to produce vegetables without the use of poisonous insecticides, will not come to look at the evidence which refutes their claims.

One book review made fun of my "laborious" cultural practices and intimated that anyone who chose to keep cats away from the garden, or to kill cabbage moths with a tennis racket, or to handpick cutworms or squash beetles, was at the very least a crackpot, though perhaps not of a dangerous type. But, mind you, I can demonstrate that such methods are less expensive and laborious and are much more effective for the home garden than the use of poison sprays or dust.

Insect populations vary from year to year between locations. Last year there were lots of cutworms and cabbage worms and relatively few cucumber or squash beetles. This year the beetles are a pest and there are scarcely any cutworms. A nickle for each cabbageworm moth inspires the kids to swing the old tennis rackets to such good effect that now they are scarcer than ever before. Beetles are easy to handpick, especially in the morning and during the mating period, and ten minutes of time each day for the past several days have brought these depredators under control. Furthermore, I have seen the sparrows feeding among the squash and cucumber vines. This small garden of about one-quarter of an acre, which outproduces any quarter of an acre that I have ever seen is, in effect, a laboratory or experimental plot, and it should provide some information concerning the control of infestations of damaging insects.

It will not provide the answers for the control of the gypsy moth or the cankerworm, for these sporadic and widespread infestations are on such a large scale that they are now beyond natural controls. Nevertheless, it will demonstrate that nature's balance will eventually check the epidemics, and that if an infestation gets out of control, it is because man himself has disturbed that balance. Whatever the eventual cure, whether man-directed biological control, or whether some other form of natural adjustment can be worked out, it must now be apparent that the broadcast use of poison chemicals for the controls of pests in nature, cannot continue if man is to survive.

In general the vegetable gardener (or any other kind for that matter) does not find himself working under benevolent circumstances, wherein kindly nature generously arranges all matters to suit his convenience. Nevertheless, we are bound to live with nature, and while some of her aspects offer enchantments beyond the powers of the poet to express, for the gardener it often seems as though she were both ill-natured and malevolent. Horace said long ago, "If you drive nature out with a pitchfork, she will soon find a way back." And so on many fronts the battle is unending.

I have been running this successful market garden for over thirty years now, and it has been my experience that the best results are obtained when one refrains from wielding the pitchfork. The less nature is interfered with the better the results, and one kind of interference which seems to be resented most is the use of poison chemicals.

The aphids which were pestering me are peculiar, for these tiny impalpable bugs are used by ants as cattle to be milked. Infestations conceal themselves as the terminal leaves of the plants curl when attacked, thus hiding the bugs from sight. A stream of ants up and down the stems gave away the show in this instance, and I promptly got after them. The aphids secrete a sticky substance called "honeydew" and ants go for this stuff in a big way, even to the point where they domesticate the lousy insects. One enemy of the aphids is the ladybug, but this seems to be a poor year for ladybugs, and in passing, I may note, a formidable year for cutworms, blast their hides. I could do a whole essay on them, but let's get back to the aphids and how to get rid of them.

Cube and derris are tropical plants (the former a legume), which have been used by natives to help them catch fish. When the pounded up plants are thrown on the water they temporarily paralyze the fish, so you wade in and pick 'em up, just like using hand grenades but much less noisy. The active principle involved is called "rotenone" and this substance is an effective insecticide, as well as a fishing aid, and therefore it is in use as a modern bug-killer which acts as a stomach poison on contact. The material I use contains 1 per cent of rotenone, 1.75 per cent of other cube resins, the balance consisting of a very finely ground powder, a mineral I suppose.

So there you have it! I'm really not cheating after all, for my insecticide is a plant extract rather than a raw chemical, and it is one that is harmless to man. At least that is what the book says; I have not eaten any, and should not choose to dust it over a dish of strawberries in spite of all the reassurances.

So plant lice present no real threat, but the drought and the killing frosts do, and unless the weather soon changes for the better the garden this year will be a source of sorrow and disappointment.

Following a typical USDA line, a typical agent, Winston A. Way, who is an Extension Agronomist at the University of Vermont, says "Biggest secret of 'Green Thumbers' is wise use of fertilizers." Fertilizers are classified as organic and mineral (for "mineral" I prefer the word "chemical," as certain minerals such as lime and phosphate rock, for instance, are not manufactured, but occur in nature.) Prof. Way says, "Arguments concerning the virtues of one source or the other are rather senseless because each contributes a different array of nutrients and possesses varying degrees of lasting quality."

He makes a good case for the use of organic (non chemical) materials, but he insists that the commercial (chemical) fertilizers are necessary for they "provide young seedlings with the readily available sources of quick acting nutrients at a critical time in their life. Organic materials never satisfy this need."

One cannot help but wonder how people got along before the erection of the chemical plants, but that is another story. It is on one simple point I call for a show-down, and that is whether or not the use of chemical fertilizers is at all necessary on home vegetable gardens; and if their use results in better vegetables.

My contention is that if the soil is in perfect condition organically the use of chemicals will not produce better crops. In order to satisfy myself on this point I conducted experiments for two successive years.

The simple test consisted of treating alternate hills of summer squash with chemicals as prescribed. In every case it was impossible to tell which were the treated hills, except there remained a possibility that the non-treated hills had the slight edge. Now, I will admit that this is not a comprehensive or conclusive test, but here is my challenge: I will permit Prof. Way, or anyone else, to test the use of chemicals in my garden on any vegetables grown there. I will await the results with the greatest interest possible. (I wonder if Mr. Way grows a vegetable garden?)

Ever since reading the very first publication of Rachel Carson's warning in the three selections from her Silent Spring, which appeared in *The New Yorker* shortly before the book was published, I have been in accord with her intentions and warnings. Even on first reading, one did not have to be a seventh son of a seventh son to predict that the impact of Miss Carson's revelations would be terrific—both on those who would attain a deepened concern with the complexities of the food chains in nature being affected by ingesting hard pesticides and on those chemically-minded interests which would fight back to save their stocks and investments.

All along one has hoped that the pressures of the great chemical companies directed toward the Department of Agriculture would be resisted. At last, a decade later, some bans have been proposed. The protest from organized chemical interests still goes on, and we are still exporting poisons to developing nations, so-called; but in this country, at least, opinions that deplore the hard pesticides are finally being heard, and in some quarters heeded.

From the day of publication of those three articles in *The New Yorker* there was a flood of editorial comment rejecting the use of chemicals in agriculture. From the very next day there began a flood of answers from county agricultural agents all over the country, following for the most part a standard line sent out by the U.S. Department of Agriculture.

These agents usually claimed that they were no "nozzle heads," and that they deplored the indiscriminate or dangerous use of insecticides. (I would prefer the word "poisons" for all of these chemicals are poisons.) Nevertheless, such a county agent insists and has continued to insist that the world would be a better place if more people used more of these poisons. This is the position he defends with rather more vigor than understanding. One I'm acquainted with frequently states, "It is a lot easier to write about 'natural control' than it is to produce food," and he may be right. But in making this flat statement he reveals that he has missed the point entirely, for Miss Carson and the rest of us have taken a stand, not *for* 'natural controls' but *against* poisoning human beings and destroying species useful to their well-being.

The fact that human beings are being poisoned by chemically contaminated food can not be refuted, and there is no more horrifying example of our abject acceptance of new poisons and our indifference to human health and happiness than is shown by the use of the drug thalidomide as a tranquilizer.

Dr. Frances O. Kelsey, an officer in the U.S. Food and Drug Administration, was enthusiastically hailed as a heroine, as well she should be, for having refused to approve of the public sale of this drug in the United States. Few people would know what has happened in Europe and Canada as a result of the use of this drug, were it not for news articles telling how Dr. Kelsey prevented wholesale horror and tragedy in this country. True, there was one other news item in the papers which told of how cleverly and with what success artificial limbs were being fitted to newborn babes, but this is a story of glorious success, not of tragical failure. Readers again have the feeling of being secure in the hands of science which can so cleverly and successfully attach an artificial arm to a newborn babe. But what of the anguish of the mothers of between 3,500 and 6,000 malformed babies in West Germany alone who have innocently ingested this diabolical concoction which science said would help them?

Thalidomide has nothing to do with pesticides as far as I know, and it is cited here simply as an example of how distorted our values have become. The drugs and the poisons and the vents from atomic power plants and the atomic explosions which science hands us we accept with alacrity, and when the dissenting voice is raised it is ignored as that of a crackpot whose sole aim is to interfere with the progress of mankind or "to frighten the public," as the publicity agents say. We positively know, on the word of the scientists themselves, that each iota of additional radiation to which humans are subjected will increase the number of children malformed at birth, but still we continue our atomic testing and still we chance accidents from atomic power plants or from the transportation of wastes to a burying ground. With the same perverted nonchalance we accept those technological devices which we are led to believe may result in the lessening of human labor, knowing all the while that these destroy our natural environment, damage our health, take our lives, and monsterize the yet unborn.

In this civilization of ours the scientists have the bit in their teeth, so to speak, and with the exception of a few who are appalled by the irreparable damage that has been done, they refuse to be brought to curb. They insist that if enough wrongs are committed, these will in the end add up to that final and glorious right which will make man's complete ascendancy over nature. How do two wrongs add up to one right? In the name of progress thousands and thousands of children are born with one arm. These we cleverly fit with amazingly efficient artificial arms, with technological devices beyond man's ability to construct a mere generation ago. So we have achieved a victory! As Sebastian de Grazia says, "Those in favor of technology consider it progress if technology manages to repair some of the damage it has done."

When the scientists have completed their structures there will be no more disease, no more poverty, no more need for labor, no more bugs, no more flood, earthquakes, hurricanes or tidal waves. In fact there will be no more human beings, for character and personality will be determined by a board of super-scientists who will have solved the mystery of life and heredity. Inhuman and identical robots will be educated by machine; reproduction will be laboratory generated; and when this once human, now monstrous growth has filled the earth to overflowing, the scientists will take over the moon and the planets. When these too have been filled, we will speed outward into space, even to the most remote of the galaxies of the Milky Way.

I am not the only one to observe that it is especially noticeable for city people, living in the constricted conditions of the city, to hold such notions and accept such fallacies without question. I say it is high time for those people—and for anyone even tempted to give credence to these notions—to get out of the city and into the country where he can reach a wider horizon, reconsider his whole set of values, and begin a new life wherein he is no longer subservient to a landlord, but is a man who can take on the main elements of his daily living as a responsibility of his own. As must be very obvious by now from what I have said in previous chapters, I believe that a new joy in living is open to anyone who assumes such a responsibility, as well as a new, more leisurely and rewarding rhythm of existence. The wider horizon will also mean that a man's propensity for maintaining these fallacies will gradually fade; he may even arrive at a clearer vision of some real truths. At least, in the country a man living on his own place can be his own boss, and he has a chance, then, of sustaining a mastery over his own life. He need not, for example, be a slave to pesticides in his vegetables, stilbesterol in his meat, chemical fertilizers for his soil, nuclear power-produced electricity in his living room, developers' decisions about what his house will look like, or the ersatz mapeline product the big-time distributors pass off as maple syrup. I am fed to the teeth with these frauds and poisons and radiations. I am also fed to the teeth with modern causes and dissents; with marches, and proposed flights to the moon, and besides these, countless thousands of petty obfuscations and self-deceits. Do you remember the old-fashioned kaleidoscope into whose tube we peered when we were young? If you pointed it toward the light, you could see how the tiny bits of colored glass arranged themselves into never-repeated designs, continually changing yet ever symmetrical, and ever beautiful. Meaningless fragments were arranged as if by magic into satisfying patterns and order.

There is now a newer device similar to the kaleidoscope which is even more bewitching and more useful, for the "teleidoscope" arranges, not the abstractions of captive bits of broken glass into some semblance of order and symmetry, but it makes use of the material objects of the external world as they lie scattered about us in meaningless disarray. Point this tube to the corner of the room where the sunlight strikes a crumpled afghan lying across a red chair and there appears on the circular screen within the tube, lovely patterns, symmetrical vertically and horizontally with exquisite colors, mysteriously changing and blending as the field is changed; each new design more incredibly beautiful than the last.

What I long for today is some sort of cosmic "teleidoscope" into which I could peer to discover such patterns and beauties as might be inherent in the apparently meaningless fragmentation of the modern world. But, alas, there is no hope in this direction, for the results achieved by reflecting mirrors, whether the mirrors be encased in a pasteboard tube or within the skull of a Dr. Pangloss, have no more reality than the cruelest mirage on a desert.

It is revealing to compare the non patterns of fragmentation with the effect of a totally ordered work like Homer's *Odyssey*. Here is shown life on a simple and heroic scale, simple and majestic and cruel. Could I take it? I'm afraid not; I could not drive the glowing stake into the Cyclop's eye, nor could I gloat over the spattered brains of the suitors as they made a mess on the marble floor. No, certainly I could not take it; but I feel somehow that this ancient concept of man—man as an integral part of nature, whose fate lies subject to the gods—is a truer view of reality than that entertained in these days, where Man is God, and Nature is to be his eager servant.

In the ancient Greek scheme of things there was order and unity, as contrasted with our Faustian world of disorder and fragmentation. We shun cruelty except in nasty ways, ways which are demeaning to man; we shudder at the thought of pain yet contrive a Belsen prison and jeer and throw rocks when Mr. and Mrs. Horace Baker pose for photographers at their home in Folcroft, Pa., where they were the first Negro residents. The ensuing picture is so charged with anguish and bitterness, that he who can bear to look into these dark faces must be moved to tears.

Somehow we have got so far off the track that we are lost.

Midway in this way of life we're bound upon
I woke to find myself in a dark wood,
Where the right road was wholly lost and gone.

Dante's Divine Comedy opens thus. We, too, are lost and we refuse to admit it. We have rejected the ancient compass and have chosen to proceed directing our way by means of devices concocted out of a philosophy which puts man at the center of the universe, employing the uses of Science to deliver Nature into his hands. With each misstep we close our eyes more tightly and require another miracle from science for the correction. We accept the doctrine of human equality, and the more things and people become the same the better we believe they become; we reject quality in objects and distinction in men. The "Common Man" is king.

Hannah Arendt in her book *The Human Condition* has said: "Power corrupts indeed when the weak band together to ruin the strong, but not before. The will to power ... far from being a characteristic of the strong, is, like envy and greed, among the vices of the weak, and possibly even their most dangerous one."

The man with open eyes is aware, as is the poet, that vice itself is weak, and a constant fragmenter:
What are the roots that clutch, what branches grow
Out of the rubbish? Son of Man,
You cannot say, or guess, for you know only
A heap of broken images, where the sun beats,
And the dead tree gives no shelter, and the cricket no relief,
And the dry stone no sound of water.

                        T.S.Eliot in "The Waste Land"
                        Harcourt Brace Jovanovich, Inc.

In these days of every imaginable food additive and of stilbesterol and feedlot imprisonment of cattle, the awful results of progress, science and technology, and of the USDA dissemination of the farm-factory view of country life, one of the greatest advantages of living on a farm is that you can raise and butcher your own beef cattle and pigs. Every November, then, butchering time will come round again, though nowadays for many in the country the rites and mysteries of hog butchering remain far-off and unpracticed.

When it came butchering time at Uncle Will's farm when I was a boy, I was even more tenderhearted than he was, and I never remember being present when the squealing beast was dispatched by a well-directed shot from the twenty-two, and the carcass bled and the gut dressed. Uncle Will hired his neighbor, Joe Wilcox, who lived down the road just beyond where the Iron Bridge spanned the Dyberry Stream, to do these bits of dirty work for him, and the butchering as well. So on the appointed morning Joe would appear, hunched up within a tattered dress coat with satin lapels, a battered felt hat pushed down over his unshorn locks, one bristly and dirty cheek distended like that of a chipmunk with an enormous cud of tobacco, carrying in his hands a murderous array of gleaming knives.

Joe was all business, and before Uncle Will and I could get the great iron pot filled with water, and a good fire going under it, here would come Mr. Wilcox driving Flora the mare down the barnyard hill, with the still smoking carcass of the hog stretched out on the stone-boat which Flora dragged behind her.

Now the two men set up the tripod while I stoked the fire in what seemed to be a futile effort to get the water scalding hot. When at last all was ready, 300 pounds or so of potential pork tenderloins, sausage, scrapple, headcheese, pickled pigs' feet, liver, to say nothing of the fat salt pork and the smoked sides of bacon and hams and shoulders would be carefully hoisted aloft by block and tackle. This gear was lashed to a gambrel stick which stretched from hock to hock, between the hind legs of the pig.

Then with much ado the great white bulk would be dunked into the water until every part had been thoroughly scalded, much as the barber prepares the wiry jowls of his customer with smoking hot towels, for all of this scalding is preparatory to the removing of the bristles. This was accomplished by scraping the hide with a device which resembled almost exactly a round-based iron candlestick. (In fact I have seen these tools purchased at country auctions under the misapprehension that they were antique candleholders.) So we all pitched in and soon Mr. Pig would be washed down and scoured, clean and white, with nary a bristle to his hide. A pig made all of meat, as one little city boy was heard to cry in joy when he saw it.

Once again Joe Wilcox took over, and as his razor-sharp knives flickered within the great cavity of the porker, Aunt Fanny hovered about with her platters and plates and bowls which gradually became heaped with the esoteric innards. Then followed the cutting up of the carcass, and the eventual smoking and salting of all those parts which could not be used fresh.

All of this happened long ago, and I can not be certain any more of the details, but I shall never forget the smell of the softwood smoke as the cold wind kept the tip of one's nose ever dripping, the damp curls of white bristles on the frozen dirt of the chipyard, the excitement and activity I loved to be part of. But best of all I remember the fresh pork tenderloins with buckwheat cakes and brown gravy and maple syrup which were served for the next Sunday breakfast.

I confess that I dwell on the events and values of days gone as though they were better than what we find in the world today. I thoroughly believe that they were. Men were a part of the nature around them, recognizing it as the awesome world they lived in. Artificialities and imitations we take for granted had not been thought of including imitation maple syrup or any of the other artificial flavorings, additives, and preservatives that fill market shelves today.

About real maple sugar, Dr. Benjamin Rush, back in 1791, in a letter to Thomas Jefferson, expressed himself thus: "In contemplating the present opening prospects in human affairs, I am led to expect that a material part of the general happiness which heaven seems to have prepared for mankind, will be derived from the manufacture and general use of maple sugar."

Reading these words today, I feel as though the famous doctor of colonial times were overly optimistic concerning the general happiness which heaven was preparing for mankind, and downright mistaken concerning the part that maple sugar would play in the hypothetical beautitude. Since the letter was written, what is commonly but perhaps not widely recognized as maple flavor, comes not from the sap of the sugar maple but from coal tar derivatives, and maple sugar, as sugar, has practically disappeared from the scene.

Nowadays the syrups which mouth-watering pictures in the magazine advertisements urge us to pour over the golden, gleaming cakes of oleomargerine which crown the summit of a pile of ready-mix buckwheat cakes contain no essence of the maple tree whatever, and the making of maple sugar plays an ever diminishing part in human affairs.

Such is the work of progress! And here there is a paradox, for the very forces of technology and mechanization which have resulted in the non-syrup and the non-butter and the non-buckwheat cakes, are now being assembled for the rescue of the maple sugar industry.

Today during sugaring season, everywhere at the sides of the roads where the snow banks appear and disappear, the ground beneath reveals, not the white blossoms and snowdrops of spring, but a forlorn and numerous collection of beer-cans and bottles, of empty pints and fifths of all colors and descriptions. Here evidence enough of the passing of that uninhibited person, who, according to Prof. John A. Kouwenhoven, a part-time Vermonter from Pawlet, "inhabits a world ungrooved by routine, a world in which he can be so mobile that he need not worry about that can blighting the landscape to which he is not likely to return ..."

Be that as it may, along with the emerging pattern of clutter and disorder revealed by the disappearing snow, the traveler could enjoy these other signs and smells of approaching spring which did delight the senses. Of these the most typical of Vermont was the cloud of steam which marked the sugar house where boiling operations were under way. Glimpses of these places nestled here and there under the trees as we sped along over the shining black asphalt transported me in time, back to the days of my youth, when I spent my spring holiday on my Uncle Will's farm in Dyberry tucked away in the hills of northeastern Pennsylvania, and helped with the sugarin'.

Nowadays the kids spend their school vacations at the spring of the year skiing somewhere or lying on a beach in Florida, and when in the north, they will quite often take a while off from the ski slopes to visit a sugar house in operation, thus getting a glimpse of a fascinating new world. But my association with the sugar house was of a different kind entirely. For me it meant hard work with muscles unaccustomed to wading through deep snow, aching when chore time came at dusk. It meant cold wet feet and shoulders sore from the wooden yoke which my grandfather had carved from a slab of basswood, and which kept the tapered gathering pails from knocking against my legs at the same time placing the burden on my shoulders where the weight was more easily borne.

When I was a kid and spring vacation came around, (this generally coincided with the sugar season in Wayne County, Pa.), my father would decide that we had better make the trip to Dyberry to help Uncle Will with the sugarin', for help was hard for him to find, and besides we could bring home some gallons of fresh syrup and some jars of soft sugar.

For me, nothing could possibly be more exciting, and after a sleepless night we would catch an early train from Elizabeth on the Jersey Central to Jersey City. Here we would take the ferry across the Hudson to Cortland Street, I think it was, where in the next dock one could get the Erie ferry back to the Jersey shore, and thus catch the one and only daily for Honesdale.

The adventures of Odysseus could not compare with this. Manhattan was more glamorous than Troy, nor could the palace of Alcinous compare in glory with the stained glass and vast spaces of the Erie terminal in Jersey City. Nor were any of the beasts or demons that beset the way of Odysseus as fearful and wonderful as the snorting steam-puffing camel-back monsters which had been tamed for our use.

What luxury of polished brass and velvet plush in these steam-heated cars, so warm and comfortable after the March winds braced on the deck of the ferry boat. We left the comfort of the Chicago Limited behind at Port Jervis, and after a wait of an hour or so, put our bags aboard the sooty and cinder-sprinkled local that ran through Lackawaxen to the end of the line at Honesdale. Here we would be met by Uncle Will with Flora, the strawberry roan mare, hitched to a buckboard providing a buffalo robe to snuggle under. It would be nearly supper-time when at last we stepped into the sweet smelling kitchen, where I would be enfolded against the ample bosom of Aunt Fanny.

The supper would be of home-made bread and butter, with soft sugar to spread on, and home jerked beef, hard as leather but sliced paper thin and creamed to go with the boiled potatoes, all washed down with the un-pasteurized, un-homogenized, un-radiated whole milk, with nothing added. Then to bed in the un-heated room under the eaves as cold as death, and the pile of feather puffs as high as the posts of the rope bed. Soon delicious warmth descended, and so I slipped away into a deep sleep lulled by the faint rustling of the corn husk mattress. Fortitude was born of the necessity of jumping out into the frigid air in the dim light of early morning, while shaking hands made short shrift of getting on enough clothes to be decent for the descent to the warmth of the living room

I can not leave Uncle Will's without first paying homage to the breakfast that awaited us the next morning. The foundations were laid on buckwheat cakes which were eight inches in diameter, cooked thin and brown on a soapstone griddle. The batter was made from flour Uncle Will had had ground from grain he raised, and a pitcher of it had stood in a warm place overnight where the necessary transformations took place under the agency of some mysterious broth made from potato peelings. These cakes, which had a sourish wonderful taste, were lubricated with home-made butter, smeared with soft-sugar and then piled up three deep. Along with these there would be an iron-ware dish with poached eggs and thin slices of home cured ham. I drool—but I must forbear!

Most significant, I think, is the disappearance of the small farm which could not afford the equipment required for tank truck milk pickup. Each of these farms had a sugar bush and they all made syrup as long as they had a contributing income from milk, but now that this is gone, they can no longer operate as maple producers. This I think is the principal cause of the decline in maple production.

Perhaps the poisons which when injected into the tap hole may increase the total flow of sap by 50%, and new methods of gas-fired arches and pipe lines for gathering sap may save the situation, but I doubt it. Two wrongs do not make one right—and the maple industry can not,

I'm afraid, be rescued by heavier doses of the technology which ruined it in the first place.

When my wife came north from the regions below the Mason and Dixon line, where no lady was supposed to submit to the drudgery of cooking (which took place in a building out back somewhere) she was simon pure, so to speak, and her only claim to culinary skill was that she could whip up a mean dish of divinity fudge. Now she showed her true greatness, for she determined to become a good cook, inspired I am sure by my mother. Whatever her inspiration, she had come to the perfect teacher and she brought to the job, devoted interest and a God-given aptitude. So I have been lucky in this way, and in many others as well, and I don't really need to be reminded of it.

But what I mean to say is that there never have been served in this house any TV dinners, that the buckwheat cakes which go with the broiled tenderloins are made from raised batter, that every Christmas season Philadelphia cinnamon buns (there are none finer) are always on the pantry shelf, that the squeak of the bread dough mixer has been heard early and late so that each of our friends may have a loaf of Christmas bread (my sister does the same), and that all through the year the Ogden table is served with home-made breads and with cornsticks (made with white corn meal ground in Kentucky).

So I could go on and on, but I find the cantankerousness in me oozing out again. We are told that as far as eating goes, never before in the history of the world has any place or nation been so blessed with as good food and in such plenty as are these United States of ours at this time. We are told further, that any old codger who in his senility makes invidious comparisons between the food of the past and that of the present is filled with sentimental self-deceit. Everything now, in fact, is better than anything that ever went before; this goes for such mundane things as food, clothing and shelter, as well as for the finer things in life, such as culture and education.

But I don't know. I think possibly the shoe of sentiment or deceit is to be found on the other foot. Where can you now find fresh pork tenderloins? Where buckwheat flour? And who will say that our bakers' bread, which is only good for making spit-balls, is better than homemade bread? And who makes homemade bread any more—a few of the young people who refuse to buy the spit-ball bread, and a few old particular codgers who refuse to give up their ties to the old better days when the smells of warm homemade bread and cinnamon buns filled the air on a crisp morning when you came in from the cold, looking for a bite to eat.

In most respects, in spite of the good things one can have in country living, the world is a mess. The advance of science presents us with frightening increases in population and with the threat of genetic damage and mutation from doses of radiation because of fallout and possible escape from nuclear power plants and the transportation and storage of radioactive wastes. Behind these ominous developments there is no evidence of a malignant group or personality; the justification for each has been the betterment of mankind. The motives have been benign, even to the splitting of the atom, with the goal of improving the human condition.

Since all of us are responsible in part for the conditions as they are today, we are unwilling to admit that there has been a deterioration in public concern, public taste, in personal propriety or in collective understanding and wisdom. We close our eyes to evidence everywhere that to increase man's material worth does not also increase his human worth and dignity. In short, it is understandably human to refuse to admit to failure. We have committed ourselves to the theory of progress. Every challenge of the idea of progress is scorned, for it is a more bitter brew to swallow than the pap of the optimists. It has been shown over and over that more of the same will not cure our ills: More powerful drugs and treatments have not reduced the ranks of the disabled; more chemicals have not increased the basic productivity of the land; more powerful pesticides have only produced disastrous upsets in ecology; more leisure has not increased human contentment or creativity; and more education has not increased human wisdom.

For decades people who have moved to the country have been saying, "I like it here because it is quiet, because you have a population not driven mad by the American mania," but in general such people have warned that they are not so optimistic or so generous as to say that everyone in a rural state is free from the 'quick growth heresy' as Sinclair Lewis and others have called it. All down the years newcomers to many a country district have cited the horrible examples of what happened in Florida, on Cape Cod in Massachusetts, on Lake George in New York, on the Texas shore, in Phoenix and around Los Angeles. They have practically always exhorted the countrypeople to preserve their priceless heritage, reminding them of "old houses that must not be torn down, beauty that must not be defiled, roads that must not be cluttered with billboards and hot dog stands." Those remarks of Sinclair Lewis point up a controversy which started long before that September day forty years ago, when the creator of "Babbitt" stood by the cluttered table as smoke curled up and the worthy Rotarians shifted in their chairs, and spoke so earnestly in praise of the state of his adoption. This controversy has been a battle between the "go-getters," who believe that any place ten times as big must be ten times better, and the escapees from the cities, who came to Vermont to "get away from it all." On the side of the industrial expansionists were the flashing swords of the promotion agencies and the editorial writers, while among the ranks of the spoil not-ers were the mighty pens of such Vermont greats as Dorothy Canfield Fisher, Arthur Wallace Peach and Harold Chadwick. And so the battle raged.

During the first years of our life in Vermont, we Ogdens were engaged in such a scramble to secure an economic and spiritual toehold in the country of our choice, that we had time for little else, but in 1935 I was sent to the legislature and forthwith became embroiled in the great Green Mountain Parkway fracas, when the lovers of wilderness and the green places put up such a fight that they were able to stop the planning and construction of a highway along the Green Mountain tops. From that time on I have been in the midst of the fray doing whatever I could to help preserve that precious and indefinable essence of Vermont, which constitutes its most important economic asset, an essence which seems to be more readily recognized by outlanders than by natives.

Our success in this state can encourage people in all states to keep up the fight to protect our heritage from destruction and desolation.

I have been told that my "writings have the flavor of jeremiads." A jeremiad is a lugubrious complaint, according to the dictionary, and while I have been contentious, have I really sounded lugubrious, and have my diatribes had the odor of peevish complaints? I doubt it.

It is obvious that many of the events and pronouncements which occur from day to day, I find to be wrong. I speak out against these stupidities and immoralities, not because I am maladjusted, unhappy, depressed, pessimistic or petulant, but because I must; and speak out I will just as long as tolerant editors put up with my cantankerousness. And in perceiving the evil, and opposing it, I suspect that I am less frustrated and harrassed by the ambiguities of our days than are many of those who reject my views, insisting that "all is for the best in this best of all possible worlds."

From where I sit at this time of year and at this time of life, I can look out across the meadows, past the neutral year's-end color of the woods, and see the western mountains, whose morning hue nearly matches the lavender of the shadows on the snow. Bromley Mountain stands there against the blue of the cloudless sky, with the white tracing of the "Pushover" trail along its Landgrove facing flank, and one can imagine that by using powerful glasses, he could see the black specks of skiers as they hurtle down the mountain.

Around on the south side, invisible from here, are the bulk of the Bromley ski trails, and from any one of these the observer can scan the slopes and trails of Stratton and Magic mountains, each but a few miles distant as the blue jay flies. The thought of these humans, male and female, young and old, many thousands of them, scrambling and sliding, laughing and falling, riding up to the very peaks and zooming down into the valleys, secure in their skill and in the ministrations of the organization which offers these trails and slopes for their pleasure, starts the wheels of memory turning.

Not so very long ago things were quite different, and but eighty years before the winter adventures which I have in mind, packs of wolves came down from these mountains and invaded the barnyards of the farmers.

About 1912, I think it might have been, Charley and Duncan Grant and I came up from the city and spent a Christmas vacation in Peru. We were on our own, and we camped out in the Grant family summer home on the old toll road, just east of the village.

In those days, no one stirred outside in the wintertime unless compelled to do so. Only an occasional horse-drawn sleigh or pung passed by the door. Our principal concern was to keep one room reasonably warm. We chose the diningroom for it had the largest stove, but still the large rug billowed several inches in the air, as the howling wind blew in through the cracks in the floor. I'm sure we were regarded with something of scorn by the natives, or at least thought to be slightly cracked, for not only did we put up with accomodations far below the countryside standard for comfort, but we mooched around outside, when we didn't have to. But we had fun.

Southeast of the village, lying in a region of hogbacks and swamps, shaped like a cashew nut, lies Mud Pond. Fascinating in summer, it was mysterious and formidable in winter, for no path led to it. It lay there in its wide valley far from any road or clearing or habitation, and we kids were attracted to it as adventurers are inevitably attracted to the realms of the unknown and unexplored. So we ploughed our way through the snow for, as I remember it, we had no snowshoes, and spent the night under the spruces huddled together beneath a makeshift lean-to of boughs before a roaring fire.

The fifty years which have passed since that perhaps foolhardy adventure have erased all memories except of the loneliness of the woods, and of the terrifying grip of the cold and the relentlessness of the wind. While there, we saw no living thing, and our safe return to civilization the next day was sweet to me. I have never forgotten the implacable and terrifying aspect that nature can assume in snow-filled woods, far from food and shelter.

How changed things are now! These mountain vastnesses once deserted even by the varying hare are now overrun by skiers, and the highways are thronged with cars. This morning I was called out to rescue a ditch-bound driver who had gone off the slippery road. The thermometer had stood at eight below, and in the few places where the swift current kept the black water open, clouds of steam arose, freezing on the brook-side twigs, while the bright sun lighted up the vapor and sparkled on the crystals.

Two loads of skiers passed me on my way; a pair of rabbit hunters got out their snowshoes and loosed their rabbit-hounds by the roadside; a last year's bird's nest sported a five-inch cap of snow overhead, and overall was the vast deep blue vault of the sky. As I returned to the house, the smoke rose straight from the chimneys in the village, and all was pleasant and peaceful; there was life and movement and nature seemed benign.

Now snow-piled villages are lively in the wintertime; the tempo of life has speeded up, and in the banks the savings accounts are swelling. All this is to the good, but the cold blasts and the blank whiteness and indifference of nature have not changed. Country people and winter sports enthusiasts all feel the grandeur of nature's winter whiteness, and life is only altered in that the sportsmen and skiers bring new activity to what was once the silent and remote fastness of the forest where we spent the night as boys. It would be foolhardy for anyone to think that by chalets and chairlifts and the snowplow or the road crew's doses of highway salt that indomitable nature has been conquered. All are part of her myriad intricacies, as it is possible to learn in the day-to-day wonders of living this country life.

Conclusion

When I closed out the previous edition of This Country Life, I concluded with a chapter called "Where Are We Heading?" and the questions raised then are perhaps even more pertinent today than they were when I first raised them. Thus, in spite of all the changes that have taken place, and even though I have new material in the two preceding chapters, I think it makes sense to pose the questions raised then once again. You will find them here in this the final chapter of the revised edition of This Country Life.

Where are we heading?

I SUPPOSE that everyone at one time or another wishes that he might forsee the trend of coming events. Actually it is a good thing that, in spite of the claims of Nostradamus, none of us are able to do so. Except for the cataclysms of nature and the strokes of fate, the future grows logically out of the present. Our beliefs and convictions, or the lack of any, determine our conduct today, and, inevitably and inexorably, the future which we are building today closes in about us. This is perhaps a long-winded and involved way of stating that the best and only way of prognosticating the future is by a critical examination of present trends in both belief and behavior. Everyone who is seriously contemplating living in the country is doing so because of a basic dissatisfaction with his present condition, and his preoccupation with the problem stems from a desire for a more satisfactory future. The problem is complicated by the fact that wherever he goes, or whatever he does, he cannot escape from the future that the world is building for him, along with the future that he is building for himself. In other words, an important factor in deciding whether or not to live in the country is not merely what is going to happen to our own lives, but what is going to happen to our civilization. It seems to me that any discussion of country living must recognize this fact. There is no escape from it. Thus I find myself confronted with the necessity in this, the last chapter, of examining present trends. Here is a subject which could not possibly be treated adequately in a single volume, to say nothing of a single chapter; and what is more discouraging, it is one requiring a wisdom far beyond mine. And, perhaps, a wisdom far beyond the reach of many of our leaders. Thus I am confronted with a dilemma: how to discuss a subject which must be discussed, not having the wit wherewith to discuss it. Of course there is no answer; the dilemma is one which I cannot solve. All I can hope to do is to indicate a few of the trends, mention a few of the thinkers who have been helpful to me, and hope that as a result you will be suspicious of the easy answers, that you will question current dogma and that you will do some thinking for yourself. Perhaps the best way to start is to list four of the most obvious and least controversial items in the stockpile of beliefs which I believe are fundamental and which form the background of our behavior. Naturally the postulates that I am about to state are in the nature of generalizations, and while they are applicable to our western civilization on the whole they are typically American in character

First and most important is the belief in the common man. I fully realize that at this point a definition is in order, and that the historical background of this belief, which was first effectively accepted in the eighteenth century, should be given. However the belief in the common man is the backbone of our democratic creed, and is so widely accepted that in this instance mere statement of the belief will suffice.

Next is our belief in progress. Here again there is little fear of being misunderstood. The premise that we have progressed since the days of our forefathers is universally accepted.

Next is our belief in universal education. This again is so widely accepted as not to be questioned. The question of what education means is another matter entirely. For my purposes I will define the word education further by stating that we mean compulsory education for all, regardless of station in life or race or creed or color or aptitude, at the public expense; and further that by education we mean book learning.

Last of the four primary beliefs is the belief that acquired characteristics can be inherited. This belief is more difficult to pin down than the preceding three, for it is more implicit in our actions than it is explicit in our thinking and talking. The term "Inheritance of Acquired Characteristics" is fundamentally derived from biology, but, to state it as plainly as I am able in human terms, it means that if you improve man's material condition you improve man. Of course it is not as simple as that, but for the purposes of this brief discussion that will have to do. In any event if you dig into the foundations of our so-called social sciences, you will find that they are built on this belief.

THE BELIEF IN THE COMMON MAN

The current belief in the common man is perhaps most evident in government. It is never possible for one to place one's finger on the exact spot in time or history when any change in man's thinking or behaving took place. All changes have been the result of many different and widely separated causes, but for the sake of brevity one can point to the year 1762 as the year significant in the shifting of sovereignty from the state as such, to the people which go to make up the state. In this year Jean Jacques Rousseau published his treatise on government called the *Social Contract*. This document undoubtedly had a great influence on the political thought of the times, and coupled with events had an effect on the trend of world history. Among other things, the *Social Contract* had an effect on the American Revolution and on the French Revolution, and subsequently upon the shape and form of the government of these United States. Our government, while based on the theory of the sovereignty of the people and "democratic" in principle, was representative in form. In other words, the will of the governed was to be expressed, but that expression was to take the form of selecting those who were to govern the state. In fact the constitution of the State of Vermont explicitly states that "The House of Representatives of the freemen of this State, shall consist of persons most noted for wisdom and virtue, to be chosen by ballot, by the freemen..." Now, with the growing belief in the common man, by insidious stages and without violent action, our form of government has changed; it has become more truly "democratic." The business of governing is still carried on by representatives duly elected by ballot, but no longer are wisdom and virtue conditions of representing the electorate. He who now represents the people is he who promises them the most, and a condition of re-election is the carrying into effect of the direct wishes of the majority of his electorate. Thus has come about the legislator who votes with alacrity on measures which propose to distribute benefits, with their attendant expense, and who votes reluctantly if at all for the measures which propose to levy taxes to pay for the benefits. Such a change could not have come about had not our fundamental conception of government changed, and this change, I submit, is a result of, as well as a proof of, our growing belief in the common man. That this belief is here to stay there can be little doubt. To what lengths it will lead us I cannot predict. There can be no question, however, but that it is responsible for such figures in our public life as William Jennings Bryan, Huey Long, and "The Man" Bilbo, to name but three of many whose wisdom or virtue might be questioned.

Just one other point in connection with this belief in the common man and one which stems from the change in our institutions as just outlined. That is that life is easy and abundant; that without effort or responsibility on the part of the individual, there shall be material security and leisure for all. At first glance this seems to be a harmless conviction, and at least a justifiable ambition. However, such a belief is worthy of critical examination, and without necessarily committing myself I would like to quote from *The Revolt of The Masses* of Ortega.

The contemporary State is the easiest seen and best known product of civilization. And it is an interesting revelation when one takes note of the attitide that mass-man adopts before it. He sees it, admires it, knows that there it is, safeguarding his existence; but he is not conscious of the fact that it is a human creation invented by certain men and upheld by certain virtues and fundamental qualities which the men of yesterday had and which may vanish into thin air tomorrow. Furthermore, the mass-man sees in the State an anonymous power, and feeling himself, like it, anonymous, he believes that the State is something of his own. Suppose that in the public life of a country some difficulty, conflict or problem presents itself, the mass-man will tend to demand that the State intervene immediately, and undertake a solution directly with its immense and unassailable resources.

This is the gravest danger that today threatens civilizations: State intervention; the absorption of all spontaneous social action by the State, that is to say, of spontaneous historical action, which in the long run sustains, nourishes, and impels human destinies. When the mass suffers any ill-fortune or simply feels some strong appetite, its great temptation is that permanent, sure possibility of obtaining everything—without effort, struggle, doubt, or risk—merely by touching a button and setting the mighty machine in motion.

As a final word on the subject of the trend that government has taken under the impetus of the belief in the common man, I would like to quote from *The Doctor Looks at Love and Life* by Joseph Collins. Dr. Collins says:

"Liberty as the architects and builders of our nation understood it, does not exist any more. Our government gets more paternalistic and centralized every year, and the time is in sight when all man's conduct will be regulated by law. It will tell him where he can go and when; what he can indulge in and what he must avoid; what he may study and what he shall not read; how he must dress and what he cannot put on or leave off."

Another impact that our belief in the common man has upon our daily lives is in the realm of understanding. Here we discover the conviction that the achieving of understanding is merely a matter of simplification or synopsis. Any subject, no matter how abstract or erudite, becomes the province of everyone or anyone. All that is necessary is that some kindly and condescending soul prepare an "outline." History, art, science, mathematics, the theory of relativity, the physics of atomic energy, music, literature, philosophy, semantics, all have been outlined, described in terms which everyone can understand, and purchased by the hundreds of thousands. Again this may be a commendable manifestation. I do not know, but it does seem that our conviction that there are easy and painless paths to knowledge and understanding is open to question.

That our belief in the common man has had its effect on standards of taste there can be no question. One has but to listen to the radio, or to attend the movies or theater to be aware of the fact. In this connection

I will confine myself to an article in *Time* magazine quoting Wolcott Gibbs as printed in the *Saturday Review of Literature*. The *Time* article, which appeared Jan. 12, 1945, says in part:

"The cinema resists rational criticism almost as firmly as a six-day bicycle race, or perhaps love.... The common level of intelligence in the world is presumably that of the normal adolescent.... Ninety per cent of the moving pictures exhibited in America are so vulgar, witless, and dull that it is preposterous to write about them in any publication not intended to be read while chewing gum."

As for movie audiences, they believe that "anything is physically and materially possible, including perfect happiness...They are a race of people who operate intellectually on the level of the New York *Daily News,* morally on that of Dayton, Tennessee, and politically and economically in a total vacuum."

This is one man's rather bitter comment after ten months as movie critic for the *New Yorker,* and however irritating it may be, I venture that few if any champions of public taste will be found to refute it. The only answer to such criticism seems to be, not a counterblast justifying conditions as they are, but merely, "so what."

It is practically impious to dismiss such a tremendous subject with what amounts to a brush off, but time and space permit no more; those who are interested will carry their studies further. In all the great literature on the subject I know of no better presentation of the case for the common man than Friedrich's book *The New Belief in the Common Man,* nor any more profound study of the whole subject than Ortega's *The Revolt of the Masses.*

THE BELIEF IN PROGRESS

The modern belief in progress is in effect a religion, and to question it is heretical. This becomes apparent if for the purpose of discussion one raises the question of the reality of progress in any intelligent and well informed group. The theology of progress resolves itself to a struggle between an evil called superstition and a good called science. Pareto in his book *The Mind and Society* has established this religious nature of the belief in progress. Because of the religious nature of the belief it is impossible to discuss the subject rationally. I will never forget the shocked and horrified surprise with which an eminent educator received my suggestion that perhaps the absolute existence of such a thing as progress could not be demonstrated.

The tangible manifestations of the belief in progress are mechanization and centralization. Whether or not the supporting theory or theology is sound, these may be beneficial manifestations. On this point I am not certain, although there is much that would lead me to question the fact. Surely in one direction the aims of technology may be scrutinized carefully by one dissatisfied with modern conditions of living, and that is in the making of effort to save effort. What becomes of the saved energy? What to do with the time saved? Surely we do not save time and energy in order that we may do nothing, it must be saved in order to do something else than that which we would be doing if we had not saved it.

Of course I know the stock answer to the question is that the time and energy saved will be devoted to cultural pursuits. But this is so fantastic that it hardly seems possible that the persons who offer such an answer really believe it. If it should be true that the saving of time and energy will result in a great outburst of cultural activities, how can it be that a culture can exist in a vacuum? By that I mean, how can a culture exist except in relation to the activities of man? The more one thinks about it, the tougher it becomes. How about the advances in medical science? Are they as real as they seem? While the incidence of communicable diseases goes down, the incidence of functional disease goes up, in almost the same proportion. Deaths from bubonic plague and typhoid have decreased to the vanishing point, but deaths from heart disease and cancer are on the increase. And all the while the population of our asylums increase. How about the high percentage of rejections from army service due to physical and mental defects? I am sure that I do not know the answers, but I am aware that the questions exist.

In the realm of man's relations with man the doctrine of progress is questioned no more than it is in the field of science, but it seems to me that there is nothing in history to match the recent, yea, current, evilness and cruelty of man toward man.

Here again there is no chance of coming to a satisfying or comfortable conclusion, nor is it even possible to more than pose the question. According to Irving Babbitt this is the age of sophistry. Sophistry flourishes on the confused and ambiguous use of general terms. In his book, *Rousseau and Romanticism* he uses the word "progress" as an example, saying in part:

Progress according to the natural law has been so rapid since the rise of the Baconian movement that it has quite captivated man's imagination and stimulated him to still further concentration and effort along naturalistic lines. The very magic of the word "progress" seems to blind him to the failure to progress according to the human law.

As an example of this ambiguity one might point to the atomic bomb, a progressive achievement in naturalistic terms, but a terrifying retrogression in humanistic terms.

THE BELIEF IN UNIVERSAL EDUCATION

It seems to me that our ideas concerning education stem from the same movement which gave birth to the concept of the sovereignty of the common man, and for purposes of simplification I believe we may refer to Rousseau as the founder of that movement. In fact by common consent Rousseau may be regarded as the father of modern education. If one studies the subject it soon becomes apparent that not only are our ideas on education and the common man derived from that which Babbitt terms the romanticism of Rousseau, but so is our belief in progress. Of this apparent community of origin, more later.

I have referred to the subject of education previously and indicated at the time that there were some doubts in my mind as to soundness of current views. There are only two points which I wish to touch on now and that very briefly. First, just what seems to be the effect of compulsory uniform education? And, second, can we eliminate from education the idea of a progressive adjustment to human law?

As to the first question I would like to quote from an article in Harper's Magazine for January 1946, written by the principal of a 350-student high school in Dover, Delaware, George Henry. Mr. Henry says:

"The state accepted long ago the principle that all pupils, bright and dull, were entitled to the same education. But the right to learn does not seem to carry with it the ability....Most parents regard passing...as a child's democratic right....Unless a teacher wishes to be picked to pieces...she cannot fail a third of her pupils, and so she passes nearly everybody....Precious little education, even for the others, is now going on."

There seems to be plenty of evidence to the effect that compulsory universal education tends to lower standards of culture, and while it fails to appreciably raise the standards of literacy, it stamps all with mediocrity. Dr. Collins on this same subject, in his book *The Doctor Looks at Love and Life* says:

"Home is still the best place for a child to learn the things that make for culture, and which no public school or compulsory education can teach him. But if those who make the home have had their individuality sapped by universal, uniform instruction, and if it has succeeded in making them one of the standardized groups, then compulsory education has reared a tree the fruit of which will be difficult to destroy."

If we presume that there is some foundation in fact for these complaints directed toward universal compulsory education, we are left with the question of what to do about it. I do not presume to try to find the answer; I merely wish to point out that there may be some reasonable grounds for questioning our belief in universal compulsory education of the type that is being offered, and to indicate my conviction that this belief is inexorably shaping the future.

Regarding the second question I quote from Babbitt again. He says:

"To eliminate from education the idea of a progressive adjustment to a human law, quite apart from temperament, may be to imperil civilization itself. For civilization may be found to consist above all in an orderly transmission of right habits; and the chief agency for securing such a transmission must always be education, by which I mean far more of course than mere formal schooling.... The notion that in spite of the enormous mass of experience that has been accumulated in both East and West we are still without lights as to the habits that make for moderation and good sense and decency and that education is therefore still purely a matter of exploration and experiment is one that may be left to those who are suffering from an advanced stage of naturalistic intoxication—for example to Professor John Dewey and his followers."

THE BELIEF IN THE INHERITANCE OF ACQUIRED CHARACTERISTICS

Here we are confronted with a belief which is more easily comprehended in its workings than in its philosophy. The philosophical or scientific angles of the belief are with difficulty connected with human angles. The battle is being fought in the biological laboratories, where a frantic effort is being made to find corroboration in science of a belief which is a basic part of our modern civilization. Thus far to the best of my knowledge, the laboratory has failed to produce the evidence which we must have if our religion of progress is to be firmly rooted in the dogma of science. One tragic incident has to do with this struggle for scientific support of our belief. The Austrian biologist Dr. Paul Kammerer, a convert to the doctrine that acquired characteristics are hereditary, believed that he had found laboratory proof in support of the doctrine, and in 1924 he published his proof in a book called *The Inheritance of Acquired Characteristics.* In this book he states:

"On the solution of the problem, whether acquired characteristics are hereditary, depends the answer to another equally important question: Does true progress of humanity exist?"

And in this book he offers proof to the world that acquired characteristics are hereditary. Shortly after the book was published—I have not the exact date available—it was revealed that certain of his experiments having to do with the pigmentation of salamanders had been tampered with by students in his laboratory. The students had injected coloration, so that the results which Dr. Kammerer believed he had achieved were falsified, and his conclusions were discredited. As a result of the disappointment attendant upon this revelation, Dr. Kammerer took his own life.

How does all this mumbo-jumbo have a bearing on us? In this way: If it is a fact that acquired characteristics can be transmitted by heredity, then if you have improved the conditions of a person's life, morally, ethically, spiritually, and physically, you will have improved the condition of his offspring as well. In this manner the world will become better and better, and gradually all evilness and cruelty and laziness and criminality will disappear. The individual no longer has any direct responsibility; society will take over; and by means of education and the social sciences the world will be transformed. To quote Kammerer again:

"This intensified responsibility rests most heavily upon the powers which direct education and government. Education, culture, schooling and training no longer exhaust their meaning where we surmised their limits to be, for not only are we benefiting the individual, but also in our disciples and pupils we improve the bodies and the minds of yet unborn generations."

You see, as Dr. Kammerer stated, this belief goes hand in hand with the belief in progress. It is a cheering belief, and one which we are tempted to accept uncritically. Whether it is a tenable belief or not, I am sure I do not know. I only know that to be consistent we should be able to produce scientific proof, and that the viciousness of our wars and the fact that children have to be taught a language tend to raise doubts.

I might go further and indicated that historically these four beliefs are truly modern beliefs, that they are the foundation upon which the structure of our modern civilization, from Nazism to Communism to Democracy stands. They are beliefs completely unheard of and alien to the civilizations of the past. Whether they be true beliefs or false, they are the ones which are shaping the world of the future. They all seem to have a common root in a point of view or a way of thinking that was first made articulate by Jean Jacques Rousseau, and which has been tagged, properly or not, romantic.

Now here is another curious thing: there is a striking parellism between the characteristics of the Romantic Movement as detailed at great lenth by Irving Babbitt in his book on Rousseau and Romanticism, and the attributes of that which Alfred Korzybski in his book, *Science and Sanity* calls "adult infantilism." The identical description of the characteristics of adult infantilism is given by Dr. Collins in the chapter of the same name in his book already mentioned. The parallels are striking, and, while it would be interesting to me to quote from Ortega, and Pareto and Babbitt and Korzybski and Collins to illustrate what I mean, I will spare the reader. Those who are interested in the subject may delve into it further to their hearts' desire. Suffice it to say that for the purposes of the present work, the existence of the beliefs which I have listed will, I believe, be acknowledged by everyone and also that their existence is shaping the world in which we live as well as the world which is to be.

CONCLUSIONS

In the foregoing I have attempted to isolate some of the basic beliefs upon which the structure of our civilization is erected, and to indicate at the same time that each one of the beliefs that I have enumerated may be subjected to reasonable questioning. I believe that many of our current problems and worries, both as individuals and as a nation, are the result of the uncritical acceptance of these beliefs.

In order to have a firm basis for decisions which have to do with the disposition of one's life it is necessary to have a direction, a goal toward which one is aiming. It seems to me that a clear understanding of what one wants to accomplish in life, and a reasoned goal, depend upon a comprehension of what we really believe and of the values which we hold to be fundamental. We cannot accomplish this without a critical examination not only of the beliefs of our civilization, but of the beliefs which we ourselves hold. I have but scratched the surface. I have hoped for no more than tc get you to think on these subjects yourself. I am convinced that they are vital, and I am convinced furthermore that any decision as to where you will live, and what kind of life you really want, cannot properly be made until these fundamentals have been considered.

No one wishing to live in the country should make the move unless convinced that the change will result in a happier and more satisfying life. For my part, the questions I have raised, and the basis they give for an evaluation of the future, offer sound and convincing reasons for country living. In the country, life seems to be more direct and normal and satisfying, and country living seems to me to erect bulwarks against the mistakes and follies of the age. Perhaps I am wrong. If what I have said convinces you that I am wrong, why so much the better. I will have saved you from making a step which you would later have regretted.

Perhaps the questions I have raised have little bearing on your problem; of that I cannot be sure. I only know that for my part I would have had the feeling that if I had ignored them I would have evaded an important part of my responsibility as a self-designated commentator on country living.

Now, whether you agree with my views or disagree, whether you choose to live in the country or not, may I assure you of my sincere desire to have been of some help, and to wish you the joy of a happy and well adjusted life, be it in the city or in the country.

Index